The Philosopher's Stone:
Seeds of a Conscious Harvest

Kirk A. Gaither II

Cadmus Publishing
www.cadmuspublishing.com

Copyright © 2022 Kirk A. Gaither II

Cover art by Kirk A. Gaither II

Published by Cadmus Publishing
www.cadmuspublishing.com
Port Angeles, WA

ISBN: 978-1-63751-359-0
Library of Congress Control Number: 2023902748

All rights reserved. Copyright under Berne Copyright Convention, Universal Copyright Convention, and Pan-American Copyright Convention. No part of this book may be reproduced, stored in a retrieval system, or transmitted in any form, or by any means, electronic, mechanical, photocopying, recording or otherwise, without prior permission of the author.

Table of Contents

Introduction 1
Closing 175
Acknowledgements 176
About the Author 177
Recommended Reading 179
Self-Help/Inspirational/Body-Mind-Spirit 185
Special Features from the coming book, "Black Grapes: The Stretching of the Stem" If Black Lives Really Matter 188
Special Features from the coming book, "AMEN: The Book of Eli" 196

Books by the Author

The Philosopher's Stone: Seeds of a Conscious Harvest
Black Grapes: The Stretching of the Stem (coming soon)
Amen: The Book of Eli (coming soon)
The Tao of Sifu (booklet) (coming soon)

Dedication

This text is dedicated to God, to sibby and honey-bunn, to the storms of life, and to all those that I harmed along the way.

"It takes the deepest darkness of night to set upon the earth to bring about the breaking of day."

"The fear of the Lord is the hatred of evil…" (Prov 8:13, TGI_Bible)

Introduction

"Personality is the distinction of the vehicle,
character is that of the driver!"

In a world filled with the knowledge of good and evil, where common sense is the master of lay people, knowing not "how" to think, but through dark arts directed in the way of "what" to think, so that they remain in the shackles of the common herd, education… "Self-education" stands as a pearl deep in the sea of simplicity. Self-education is the mountain that leads a man's mind to question, and the ability to question without opinion is the door to wisdom where with introspection into the deep recesses of one's own heart, character is born. With the birth of character, the weeds of ego begin to be choked out and the personality stilled and washed clean so that it serves as a clear windowpane to the soul of man. With the maturation of character, one begins to pierce the veil of the tree of death in the world and in oneself, leading man to the gift of good sense where the questions of who, what, where, and when are superseded by the question of why and ultimately of HOW. To ask how is to examine the pieces that make up the whole of a thing. It is to understand what is beneath the hands and face of the clock; to know what makes the clock tick.

"The fear of the Lord is the hatred of evil," and to hate evil is to gain insight; to discern people, places, and things as they are in contrast and in distinction from what they appear to be. When a man has the courage of humility to ask "how," he not only begins to evolve in the capacity of his mind but also comes to the seat of the judge where he is gifted with the challenge of creating his thought unadulterated by the opinions and perspectives of others. It is here where he can pose questions from his core in relation to things as they naturally are, and by this leads men from the lower rungs of commonality into greater realizations of themselves.

The author has herein posed questions for the reader to ponder in the recesses of his/her own heart with the hope that each may be led into the halls of wisdom and thus to a higher realization of themselves, and a union with the Creator. It is found in the Holy Bible, "Seek ye first the kingdom of God and His righteousness and all other things will be added unto you." To seek the Lord and His righteousness is to shun evil, evil things, and the wrong path, which is harmful to and infringement upon others, selfishness, pride, arrogance, and the forwardly in tongue. Through this door are the muddy waters of the world sifted through the soul of man so that his vision is cleared and he sees things as they stand in truth. The only real way to observe a thing is with penetrating eyes. To not only view the outside but to see the contents at the same time, and also to discern the motive, intent, and instruction of that thing. To truly see is to view something totally, inside out at the same time. As long as the earth shall bring forth thorns and thistles the vision of man shall be challenged by the real illusion of evil, and wickedness. So then man must toil with even his very ability to see and to know a thing in truth. He must ponder things and the questions and words that have been put toward things before him, and let his hands help his mind understand by the hands-on experience of things until his mind reaches a place where he no longer must experience all things to know what they are but to know he absolutely must question still.

    The Chinese bamboo tree is an amazing thing. Once the seed is planted it will be around 18 years before a single twig breaks the surface of the ground, and once that single twig greets the rays of the sun it will strengthen and stretch itself 18 feet or so toward the warmth of the heavens in a single year. What is interesting about this process is that in all those years after that single seed was buried in the soil without a single sign of its presence it was alive and growing, stretching itself deep into the soil of the earth for water and nutrients. By the time it shows itself above ground as a babe in the sunshine its roots are strong, long, wide, and many. Let man take time with understanding. Let him search and seek in the way of what was before him. Let him enrich himself so that he might be useful to the whole of creation and have the strength to weather the storms of adversity that will come to him to test the resolve of his heart and the sincerity of his soul's cause. Ponder this text! Chew it, digest it, and figure out what you figure. They have been set out for your growth and that the peoples of the world might advance in our way rather than decline into the grips of dilapidation… Be blessed and enjoy!

1. Hate not thy brother for his troubles whatever they are, but love with understanding and wisdom because though you may have been through a hundred births, he may have only existed for three or four though his flesh now in this space of time be of greater age than yours.

2. Remember that time lies in the belly of eternity.

3. Any man, having truth on his lips shall be hated by the world because the truth is accompanied by conviction.

4. Philosophy: be it, the story and tell of the search.

5. By the value of the thought shall a man be placed above or below, for there are many in mass who ascribe not to know.

6. You are not only alive as you live in the hearts and minds of others… To what degree be thy favor and blessedness?

7. Befriend everybody but do not make everybody your friend. Let enemies place themselves in such a position and do all things in their proper moments!

8. One only knows the truth as he has lived it.

9. If I do not perfect my know in the knowledge and art of ME, I shall only be a hindrance to others.

10. Worrying about the affairs of others shall only leave you unsatisfied with yourself.

11. What doesn't live in the mind doesn't manifest in the body.

12. Troubles come and troubles go but opportunity is rewarded to those who optimistically think through problems.

13. A man shall only know what he lives and by his living, the world shall know if he knew how to live.

14. Whoever's life has not gathered unto him a philosophy of how and why to be, knows not the way of truth.

15. Why should I ask a question to receive an opinion when I can know by the fruit of my labor and the drive of my effort?

16. A chattering tongue is the business of a lazy man, having for himself no produce of substance.

17. The mind of man shall reach madness and break the sea of confusion when his feet have carried him beyond the borders of his thought.

18. Of all things having peace in the mind is the most crowned of achievements.

19. Material or spiritual?; the body or the mind? Whichever be the false and the reality, after careful consideration I have come to determine that I shall enjoy both because these are both a part of me. So that I am not at fault before the creator I shall redeem my time by living and learning with all the faculties of my body and my mind respectfully, and this to my heart's delight.

20. Do not focus on a single point within the whole. Focus on the whole as a single point.

21. Forget about yourself and follow your opponent's movements, then penetrate the voids. No plan is the plan!

22. The heights that you're willing to reach for shall be the markers for your entail.

23. If you can't recover quicker than it took you to take the risk, then avoid the risk.

24. To know God simply focus, and that on God.

25. When you don't know how to learn you always have to start over.

26. Success is just past the place of failure.

27. To know God is to be God in part.

28. One must know that the nature of life as life is, is like looking at the moon's reflection upon a body of water while unaware that the reflection is not the true object viewed, and at the same time unaware of the body of water until the moon is grasped at… At once the reality of the illusion is discovered and broken, and the mind expands at the new awareness of the water, its motion, at the revelation of the true position of the moon, at space and time, and at the phenomenon of a reflection and the water's reflecting quality. Life is a continual newness from what is and was… birth and death to birth and death!

29. To know the truth you must first hate evil.

30. Even the ignorant will be granted a place, but authority and honor are only given to those who have strived in the way of knowledge and held themselves accountable to it.

31. To be a man of your word and to always practice what you preach is to live undivided.

32. When you fall down don't give up, get up!

33. Why fight over differences when these are what make us who we are individually?

34. To answer "How am I leading?" is to ask "How am I serving?"

35. Play not for the love of the game, but to win the game.

36. To have power is to empower.

37. Good opportunities are among those that come while great opportunities are those you create.

38. The more game you have, the fewer games you play.

39. To take pressure off of others and oneself is to master life and all its parts, conditions, and circumstances.

40. To continue to step forward is to be opposed the more and to receive more and more of the earth under your feet.

41. The truth and reality of your vision, the strength of the will, and the power of your destiny shall be measured in the opposition to that call.

42. Much learning builds me up to the statute of others. Much decreasing strips me down to the whole of myself.

43. Death I defeated at the birth of a child. Life I shall champion at the passing of my own flesh.

44. The way to "empty the cup" is to not hold things but instead to let things pass on, much like the waters of a river flowing into the sea or like fruit falling from the tree.

45. One should not seek to simplify the complex nor to make complex the simple, but rather to comprehend what is as it is. In this way, one sees the fruit, the seed, and the very manifestation and process of creation's course together and at once. This is to observe with an empty mind free of distraction and opinion.

46. In life we should seek to grow conscious of the negative in order to return to the unconsciousness of the positive so that we as mankind in creation again evolve from the top.

47. When I look at others to measure myself, I'm confused. When I look at my past to measure my growth, I'm at peace, focused, and blessed. I've decided to move forward!

48. Morals are not how one should act with others, but how one should act with oneself.

49. Losing is so great because it's the foundation from which winning is achieved.

50. The walk of the journey is only enjoyed by those who anticipate the climb.

51. When water is in the sunlight it sparkles. When water is in the dirt it is muddy. Joined with salt it is salty and when it runs over the rocks it is sterile. Like water, I will be whatever is needed of me to help others along as long as it benefits us both to strive together.

52. I have decided by my struggles and declared by my efforts that… "I am opportunity!"

53. Know what you know so that you can prosper from what you think.

54. Get up! Feeling sorry for yourself only says you've fallen twice.

55. No blaming! No whining! No complaining! No insulting! No boasting! No bragging!... Saying no to all of these things exercises my self-worth.

56. If conversation is the rule of the day, and actions speak louder than words, strive to always be found speaking and doing good things, things that bless others so that all who hear and look upon you grow in knowledge, wisdom, and understanding. By this, your name shall live.

57. When you worry about, doubt, and anticipate… Let it go, that it may be had in its proper time.

58. People get what they want when the work of their limbs mirrors the desire of their heart.

59. Not until my own eyes bear witness to the things my ears have heard, and my hand tests the quality and sureness of such, and my understanding approves the three as one and good, I shall trust myself alone to God and me.

60. The beauty in flaw, it's so perfected that it's truly an awe.

61. How can man grow or know if anything in a thing is good or bad, or even know a thing if it can be known if he never questions?

62. To live discreetly and censored is to predict the weather by controlling the sky.

63. Worry will cease when yesterday and tomorrow cannot be found on the tongue.

64. I can only help myself and advance as I help others to do the same because this alone is the definition of achievement.

65. Should I be so irresponsible with the measure of my mind in which man operates as to not give it to God? By my tithe of responsibleness, He shall ignite my brain to its full capacity. Or is the Father so foolish as to cause man to operate in full measure without acknowledging Him!

66. He who has entered the plain of intuition by becoming the master of karma (reaping only what he has purposely planned to harvest in his method of sowing seed) in the art of thought and the spoken word… Master-mind!

67. If one person speaks a word it manifests eventually, but if a multitude speak the same word, it manifests NOW.

68. Conversation rules the nation but actions speak louder than words!

69. I'd rather worship a God that I can't see who takes care of the things that I cannot see than to serve a king that I can see, and from whose eyes I can hide.

70. Because all that I give is directly tied to that which I receive, I shall strive to manage with wisdom my handouts.

71. Reward yourselves with the pardoning of thy mistakes. With humble apologies do all that thy must, to see that others carry not with them to slumber and rest, anger because of thee.

72. To question by the utterance of the tongue is good, but to ask what thou seekest in quiet meditation is rule. Let all that passes thy ears and thy eyes, thy skin, and thy nostrils, and even that which touches thy lips be asked of wisdom and the key of life that thy may learn to go in and know the voice of God.

73. Who can have confidence but the curious! . . . . . . Those who search, question, and read.

74. The loss of money is nothing next to the loss of a good reputation

75. If anyone knows a thing let him celebrate the question, however, being discreet and discriminate with the answer, ever careful, that he not cast his pearls to swine.

76. The greatest and quickest way to crush your enemy and conquer in absolution is to let him win first.

77. To make an enemy a servant, praise him and exult his name before men.

78. A man shall know himself when he has decided who he is.

79. Appreciation, satisfaction, and the heights of stewardship comes where you have to fight to obtain what it is that you desire to hold.

80. Knowing first, that a little good outweighs a multitude of evil; if you set the direction of things in the spirit first followed by the mind, and the spoken word, the body and all other things in the physical realm must surrender to the navigation set in the fields above.

81. Goals, long-term: set without the short means "I stumble!", short-term set without long-term means "I'm lost!"

82. What good are all the smiles and the cries if I will never be remembered when I die?

83. I don't stick to plans. I make them, and I make them again.

84. "The know" is in the Beginning.

85. The world belongs to the philosopher's because they shape the beliefs of the masses.

86. Whatever a man does not wish to make a habit, he should cease to do.

87. Question! Is God your God when He says no and can't be found?

88. In all his majesty, and though he be king of the jungle, what lion in the might of his strength would dare to wake a sleeping dragon?... some things are better left alone!

89. The future of a man is revealed in whatever he stands to gain or lose in measure of his desires.

90. For a man to hold his brother accountable in his daily dealings and speech at a standard of goodness and gentleness toward all is the highest order of keeping thy brother.

91. In all your strengths and weaknesses as a man, in this moment will you stand or fall?

92. The toil of the pen unties the knots of the mind.

93. When you have considered all of yourself on the stage of life from beginning unto the present moment, mind, body, soul, and the destination desired, only one question need be answered. Are you winning or losing?

94. Foolishness! I say unto the student who looks upon the pastimes and interests of the master, seeking to make these his own in hopes to gain enlightenment. Have you not, I ask, considered the toiling with life in which you must bear alone and the fact that from one's own trails shall arise his own interests and pastimes?

95. Freedom means minding my own business.

96. As long as birds choose to eat out of the hand they will continue to sing from inside of the cage.

97. Today is where yesterday met the possibility of tomorrow in real time.

98. When you decide what kind and how many fish you want to catch, you'll know when, where to fish, and what tools are needed to succeed.

99. In solidarity I have learned the art and necessity of being used. In being used I have learned the gift and rest in solitude. These two should walk together, so that one may bless and be a blessing.

100. In order to view debt and the indulgency of any peoples correctly, let us look first to the peoples' foreign credit and second, to their storehouse and fields of prosperity and production, and lastly let us look at the world's current and projected need of those things, and also at the rate in which all of these are yielded.

101. To focus on "past and future" leads to illusion, for these only exist in the flesh. Let all things be assessed in the now. Surely the past and the future have attachments of doubt, worry, anxiety, envy, anger, resentment, and every form of evil against thy neighbor, even flattery and deceit, but the now is free.

102. To be great among gods is to be humble among men.

103. If the gods be helpers of man, how can men gain any greater favor with them than to be of service to his kindred? If man's countenance is lifted and if praise is given to those who aid and assist, think not that God or His league of angels delight in any different.

104. The inner depths of man, be it weakness or strength, is visible if we only dare to listen.

105. It's not because a man has striven that he shall gain my respect, but that because he strives, he shall receive it.

106. The way of authority in anything is through trial and error, rigorous preparation, and by the passing of that thing through all of the faculties of oneself.

107. Success is the persistence and prudence of preparation.

108. True salvation comes with knowledge and understanding, for this is the seed and the fruit, the door and the path which one's feet tread upon if thy eyes only look to see, and thy ears listen to hear.

109. I do not look to escape my pains, nor do I seek to ignore the destruction of my life. What I strive to do is to scrutinize the damage and rebuild the bridges I have destroyed in my life, and to serve as instruction to those who come after me so that they do not lay their hands against themselves.

110. Life is about the struggles rather than the victories, that wisdom might be a reward unto man.

111. Forget about right and wrong, good and bad, and only do what is right that you may eat of the tree of life.

112. To overcome oneself, the world, and all its evils, is to master knowledge and understanding which is the fear of the Lord, and to know the holy one, for this is where all things end and begin.

113. Let men bond not over things of folly, but over knowledge and truth; over labor and the things that render a harvest in goodness and righteousness and are pleasing to God so that the family and the land, and all thereof be blessed by the Lord.

114. If we are to live, let our focus be on the good things that produce joy and prosperity for others rather than ourselves, for our own needs for such things will become the focus of others at the degree to which we give.

115. The battle which rages within oneself between good and evil is best untangled one knot at a time, where understanding and instruction stick to the soul over time rather than to take a quick thrust at the rope with the sword, where the wisdom in the toils of the struggle are forfeited in trade for the pleasure of temporary ease because in long-suffering are the deceits of the heart ironed into love and the knowledge of God matured in man.

116. You cannot be fooled nor manipulated by what you know you know when you know that what you know, you know not.

117. If God is in me, should I not be still and listen to myself?

118. I shall approach all things as a student so that I leave them as a master.

119. Persistently diligent practice rewards the tongue with authority's speech of influence.

120. I shall only know what to expect from a man when I have asked him what he expects from himself.

121. Mastery shall be my way of life, by the application of all my faculties in thoroughness in every venture, that I may obtain a seat among the great and humble.

122. To recognize is to be informed. To perceive is to be experienced, but to instruct with understanding is "to be!"

123. Why stop at being thankful when it blesses the giver to show appreciation?

124. Natural!... is absent additives.

125. The sun and the moon be only distractions until you know the purpose for which you were created.

126. If I should stand you next to myself, it is because I trust that what you do while standing here will be the best thing for us both.

127. I shall not order you. However, by my silence, you will direct yourself to either stand or fall by the contents of your own mind. By your positioning of yourself my tongue shall be guided on how to speak.

128. When what you believe has become what you do and teach, then you have become that thing.

129. There is neither good nor evil, neither right nor wrong. There is only what you do and do not do, and the harvest thereof.

130. If God made me to enjoy the best things in life, I am not sorry that I want them.

131. I have never met a gossip monger who was not guilty himself of transgressions.

132. Until a man learns to learn, folly shall continue to be before and after him.

133. Unless one breaks out of his own way, he shall never learn what he thinks he knows.

134. Emotions!... nothing be it more contagious.

135. Let all the things that a man does be done inside, seeking and acknowledging God, that he may be established in his way and blessed in his labor, rather than taking things to God that He might measure and refine, that he may not transgress in the way.

136. Let a man's knowledge always outweigh his desires and he shall overcome every obstacle.

137. AMRAK: "To consciously cause an effect to effect a cause."

138. When a "man in God" arises, the world has a choice. They can say "blessed" or they can say "cursed," but whatever they say shall be their own reward.

139. To forget time is to realize eternity.

140. When the one who seeks releases his grasp of all that is outside of himself, he shall find within him his own way.

141. Outside of cliches and stereotypes where opinions and judgments do not exist, you shall find the door to enlightenment and the power to become forever present.

142. Upon the rebellious, who secretly mourn with sorrows within their hearts, shall the Lord bestow mercy and grace, but woe unto those who turn from the way, for when men get serious in their way against the Lord, God shall surely be serious in His way against them.

143. I shall, in every way, with all my abilities, put away the past so that I forever live today.

144. If all things constantly evolve in relation to all other things, only "now" shall fill my mind, and now from moment to moment.

145. Who knows God and how He is found but he who has received from God a new name?... the name of his own being in God, united as one.

146. Of the two great commandments of love given by the anointed one, "To love the Lord your God with all your heart, mind, soul and body," and, "To love your neighbor as Christ loved the church," let man by wisdom reach the first with diligence, by constantly applying the second.

147. Do not seek knowledge, wisdom, and understanding into the ways of man, nor of the gods, nor things unseen, but rather let man seek to without condition love, yet the way to seek is to give of yourself that which you wish to find.

148. I'm so street smart I'm book smart, I'm so book smart I'm street smart… O' the wonders of simple understanding!

149. One thing provokes fear and joy in the hearts of man above all, depending on their measure of selfishness… Honesty!

150. The eyes shall only be open to see God for oneself when the hands and feet move revealing the Father's character to others.

151. The deep darkness in man's eyes exists because he chooses not to give the love of life unto his neighbor.

152. If I had to choose to live among enemies only, or friends alone, I should choose to reside among my enemies because by this my vision would be clear, and I would not be led astray by the deceit of man.

153. Why should man be confident in himself when God is his creator? This should not be so! All the days of my life I shall be confident in my God alone, for in Him am I strong.

154. I'd rather be with an enemy whom I can make a friend than with a friend who will make himself an enemy.

155. When God requires what He gave… so be it!

156. Be not blinded by spoil, for thy labor and the sweat of thy brow be the root of all prosperity.

157. However, you do it, it is right!

158. Peace is a substance created, not found.

159. Why have to apologize for what you say when you can manage your words?

160. Good, bad, right, and wrong are not so and do not matter until a decision is made.

161. Whatever you want in life; who and whatever you decide that you are, wherever you choose to go… "create it!" It is totally up to you.

162. True riches reside with the one who casts no projections, for he finds usefulness in all things as they are today.

163. If you know yourself, everything else you'll figure out.

164. If it's worth something, brand it because everything of value has a name.

165. To all that wonder and ascribe to know, a man to himself is father and son.

166. In all things there lies two roads; contentment and covetousness. All of a man's circumstances are rooted in one of these.

167. My most honored and most deserving profits come when I share myself and invest in me doing so.

168. I gain wealth and become rich when I increase my value by giving of myself.

169. To know the quality and the art of a man with a woman look to how he orders his finances.

170. Everything I say is better the next time you put your eyes to it.

171. Better to be ignorant with a settled stomach than intelligent and hungry.

172. O' how blessed! And what peace it brings to live with few words.

173. It takes the deepest darkness of night to set upon the earth to bring about the breaking of day.

174. I deny anyone power over me by the wrongs they inflict because I have chosen to forgive and not hold them at fault, nor responsible for their transgressions against me.

175. To he who walks not contrary to, but in sync with his tongue, his words shall surely come to pass.

176. I do not have the power to give time away, but I do have the ability to take it.

177. Better to never have been born than to have loved and be forgotten.

178. Consider not, "to be or not to be," but only what to be!

179. Self-governorship rewards with the crown of the crowd.

180. Through working out my own salvation, having with me the divine right to choose, I have come to know that I am what and who I decide to be.

181. To know the size and stature of a man, consider what he makes his enemy.

182. Let the journey abroad be only to please others with showers of exaltations and the interest of them, while thy solitary is to do likewise with thyself, because only in me can I know and find me.

183. Though the hand is quicker than the eye, it shall never move unseen by the spirit.

184. Fear is not when you decide to believe.

185. If you aren't reaping while you are sowing, you're not planting enough seed.

186. Seduction is much a sport. A game of offense and defense where one is only enjoyable in the company of the other.

187. Greatness shall only be the lot of those who take time with purpose.

188. The requiring of a defense with an offense to win turns hobbies into sport.

189. He who cannot say "no" to himself shall never see old age, and his name shall die with him.

190. After I have let my mind and my heart travel, asking, seeking, and knocking in search of many things, I shall shed from myself all things and stand in observation of the world, content to be none and all.

191. A compliment, a gift, and an interest shall always do one the blessing of being welcomed and the courtesy of many favors with men and women, rich and poor, and shall always remain the foundations of a good courter.

192. Affect each other with smiles and let that be the energy that gives each of us the strength and aspiration to overcome any obstacles we face.

193. Let it be known by all mothers, fathers, brothers, sisters, and all other relations, that at the end of the day, you can only call those family whom you have taken an interest in and delighted with attention.

194. Foolish thing it is to seek peace when it is not the gift you bring, for man shall only find for himself the things which he has cast abroad.

195. I shall stand when I consider my ways, but I shall stumble and sink into the grave when I worry myself with the ways of others.

196. Constantly digging in the past shall keep my feet from forward progress. First, decide your future and then your history will be revealed. All things begin in the now.

197. There is a difference between awake and alive, and between dead and asleep. Be therefore diligent with light and prudent with the word to know the difference.

198. If you desire to give birth… speak the word and move to see it.

199. If you want to find the worst bad guy, seek out the best good guy.

200. I have found nothing to possess more beauty than priceless giving.

201. You never get away with anything at all. Things simply tend to catch up to you when you can't afford it.

202. Because I am a brand, I will invest in myself to increase my value because nobody's buying worthlessness.

203. You can play with your life and make living a debt to yourself or you can work and have recess as a reward.

204. A man without restraint is a man without a future.

205. Opinion! Be it the spouse of judgment, and they should not be.

206. Realization comes only in exercising.

207. Whoever chooses not to be a king or a queen shall be made a slave.

208. To believe is to obey and honor.

209. Those who seek pleasure shall never find the truth, but those who search out suffering shall see God.

210. Not when you're down, but only when you strive to stand alone and rise from the depths of misery shall you know the truth in every man.

211. Experience is measured by the depth of wisdom. Why fish with a rod when I can cast a net?

212. Wisdom is to see the unseen before the unseen is seen. Instruction is giving the unseen its course of direction in the seen, while it is unseen so that wisdom proves itself useful.

213. To be a mystery to the carnal mind is a revelation to the spirit. To be alive in the flesh is death unto God. Whatever I speak, being in Christ shall render death unto the mortal and life unto the ghost; and this to the glory of God.

214. Too many yeses and I shall feel entitled, too many nos and I shall feel neglected. How blessed is he who has learned how to receive without asking of another?

215. All that I have, and that which I don't, is enough, for this is my allotment.

216. A person's endurance should be measured in their state of rest.

217. Only those with experience behind them and vision ahead are in possession of desire and drive in the now.

218. Though I cannot speak, my legacy demands that I work hard.

219. The best trails are those heavily laden with obstacles.

220. What is a good journey without roadblocks?

221. If I shall be rich in this life or in the next should not concern me. All that I consider is how much I enrich others today.

222. The ugly in me I dare not to see, for I am beautifully and wonderfully made, and however that I am, this is all that I shall be.

223. A mill stone to crush or a cloud to lift be wisdom unto men, and man shall decide their own way whether they shall rise or fall by the measure of God.

224. A master should never be so foolish as to reveal unto a student while the student is his pupil the things endured which have brought him to mastery.

225. To look at every man as my superior, and to treat them as such, with respect and conviction is to be the ultimate leader and master of influence.

226. Iniquities stored up in the heart against a neighbor is a shackle of fear of thy neighbor's face.

227. I shall be master of all when I have learned to serve myself with complete love.

228. The tool that causes one to change direction… "Question!"

229. The extent of man's struggle lies in his ignorance, but with education comes freedom and options.

230. How should I apologize if I have thoughtfully considered my brother with love first?

231. I cannot fail when I have decided that I am a winner.

232. All that I have received from the Lord I shall render unto man all the days of my life so that all be well with my soul.

233. As I journey towards the giver of life, compassion shall follow me and reverence shall lead.

234. Pleasure found outside the cycle of work is only waste.

235. Whoever indebts the world with kindness shall never receive charity, but rather their just due.

236. If I haven't given what I wish to keep, then I haven't given at all.

237. Why should man fear when all things concerning him are creations of his own mind!

238. The only way to overcome and conquer is to create and build.

239. What I have prepared in good faith, that I shall trust.

240. If you fear the unknown, it is because you have failed to create your circumstances to fill the void space.

241. Whatever ideas drive the hand to build, having been created, is the reality.

242. Once a thing has been mastered in any direction, the only thing left to do is teach that which you know and move on.

243. The pinnacle of education is that others bear the burden to build the structure in my mind's eye.

244. Some people are live yet motionless, while others are busy but dead. To live in motion is to be alive and lively!

245. A fall is only a stumble when you get back up.

246. First be known for wisdom, then for wrath, and then for charity.

247. Every moment should be used to forecast, navigate, and establish the next moment, for you are only what you practice.

248. The grass is definitely greener on the side where people apply opportunity.

249. To measure the extent and extremity of victory and/or failure tomorrow consider the benefits of today's blessings.

250. Motive and intention are the keys that unlock or lock the gate to the unlimited intuitive method.

251. Prayer is nothing where effort is in lack.

252. After much tribulation and abandonment, after much care and rebellion, I have come to know that family is what you do and not who you are.

253. If I am broke then my lot must be poverty, but if I enrich myself then myself shall be rich.

254. To discipline the mind and body against the pleasures of the flesh is to supersede in the ability and strength of responsibility, exercised with those pleasures resumed, giving birth to moderation.

255. When you bless others in your mind's eye, others will bless you with the hand and tongue.

256. Let her who seeks companionship not strive against her neighbor in her heart.

257. Whenever one stops possessing things as owner and starts to be a steward his coffers shall overflow with abundance.

258. It is the duty of every man to gain control of his faculties for lack of control and indulgency of one area breaks down the construction of the whole the longer the beast festers.

259. In the mind, on the lips, and in the eyes of others, who am I?... Considering such, I shall encourage health and joy in others.

260. To be thorough and sure, I shall hold myself accountable in my judgment.

261. In Life! Whatever it is, was, or could be… show up!

262. A man is truly free once he has released the world from his grasp.

263. Sight receives understanding from the eyes' enrichment of discernment and instruction when the mind is filled with knowledge.

264. People only love you when you're benefitting them.

265. The beginning never starts first.

266. Whatever this man shall become, I won't struggle or hesitate to be, because I have labored and toiled, and prepared myself vigorously to be that.

267. It's not what you do, nor is it how you do what you do, but the whole measure of returns lay in why you do what you do.

268. Everything in creation is everything else in creation, yet in another form, another existence, another reality, and experience on another frequency, existing at the same moment as everything else, interacting and affecting all other things at the same time.

269. Let those in haste learn a truth, let the sluggard and resting receive life. Time has neither legs nor wheels but is fastened in its place. It is the souls of men who are in motion, passing through time never early and never late, but on time according to our works or the lack thereof.

270. Dear man, have you not yet understood that in all your ways, with your many parts, that you are the thoughts of God?

271. Familiarize yourself with others of like-mindedness and character rather than skin color, because when the eyes are closed, we are all one shade.

272. Individuality is exercising the right to be yourself in the way you are despite the crowd.

273. Better to have no reputation than to have to uphold the weight of one already written in stone.

274. Sometimes you have to quit being you to be yourself.

275. As the battle waxes strong on the exterior with danger escalating on every side, let the man gaze the more upon the virtue of his own heart for a decision, holding fast to his vision for peace and presence.

276. Love is the choice to exalt and give your best to someone else because giving, yielding to, and serving them brings the best out of you.

277. In the measure of war, that the extreme is the reward, let the pen precede the sword.

278. Value is only found on the inside and must be projected outwardly.

279. Let the clock be the ideal in the proper construction of war and peace.

280. To truly know a thing, do it!

281. Danger does not exist where one has decided to conquer.

282. To pierce the veil of your opponent's mind, look to his morals, for here lay his points of internal warfare.

283. A great father leads his son with boldness from a reflective mind that his son may wax strong in confidence and consideration of others.

284. Give morals to the soldier to inflame his combat but let the general who aspires greatness to be free of them to strengthen his battles.

285. If God's blessings are what you desire, first grasp His attention and make blessing you a desire He approves by giving Him praise.

286. If I want to find what I'm looking for, I've got to see it first.

287. I know when I need not know, but when I need to know, I know nothing.

288. One can never understand and know what he does not search out.

289. In the game of show and tell, the words are second to the action, explaining what the eyes have already been exposed to. If this isn't your life, you must talk too much.

290. If God be within you, birth Him. If you be in God, serve Him. If you be a son of God, cultivate yourself so that the world may know the love by which it was created.

291. The road to prosperity now and later, I seek. What good is it to be in possession of abundance of booty but poor mentally, spiritually, and emotionally? And how is it blessed to be rich spiritually, emotionally, and mentally but lack bread upon thy table? If I should seek the unseen, I shall look through the glass of that which my eyes behold.

292. By labor light is given to the eyes and understanding to the mind of man.

293. It is better to have a bad name than no name at all because even the bad names were known by the people.

294. If life and death truly reside in the tongue, then I shall strive to elevate and exalt others with my words so that my days are many and blessed.

295. To the wise: A bad reputation is the birth and testimony of a great name.

296. With the poor is a bad name but with the rich is a good reputation.

297. A true friend makes it her duty and responsibility to cultivate and know her whom she calls friend, even to her own hurt so that she knows and is, at all times, able to be a blessing through meeting her friends' needs.

298. The key to make one's path; the oppositions and opportunities, expose themselves before ever taking one step on thy way, is to practice one's steps in the direction you plan to go with severity.

299. Opening up is a job belonging to oneself.

300. To get to the top of the mountain you must climb. Once you reach the top you must build.

301. Whatever thing it is that you fear, that thing also attack.

302. Never give advice without a price because man, by nature, uses and abuses; exploits and destroys all things that are offered for free. From the beginning, men only constrain themselves when they pay a price.

303. Who is it that pouts but the man who knows not that everything in which he lacks and others possess is but his own if he only claims and receive those things for himself with his labor and service for those who have them.

304. The enlightened mind is not "what you know," but how you have become what you know, and because of what you know became no-thing.

305. Friendship is a thing earned and acquired, never tried.

306. Perfection is impossible without scars.

307. To convert sociology into common sense; to transmute knowledge into understanding; to discern the wisdom of culture in every arena and no arena, to embody the instruction of wisdom, justice, judgment and equity, and to breathe these things simultaneously is to know master and student.

308. To live is to appreciate.

309. To know Christ is to realize oneself in God and God in oneself.

310. The ending of all selfishness is knowledge, and the beginning of truth is ignorance.

311. To be alive is free, but to sleep is much costly!

312. Let her who is unkind manage her mind!

313. If the mind is the master, then choose carefully what you think.

314. When my past becomes beneficial, my now becomes blessed and the morrow is thoroughly considered today.

315. I am power, I am wisdom… I am love!

316. Knowledge is a shield against conflict and a sword against circumstances, for in life, only the learned shall live.

317. Never shall one enter into the kingdom of God until the kingdom of God is found within such a one.

318. Let the experience in a man be seen and felt so that its message in words be spoken by those who bear witness.

319. It is the blind and foolish who imagine heaven in the hereafter and enjoyeth it not in the now.

320. What is darkness but a question in need of the right answer!

321. If a man wants to see different, he should be different.

322. To do kindness unto thy neighbor, to extend patience and understanding unto thy enemy in a spirit of humility and love is to work the highest miracle and the grandest wonder.

323. Wisdom is not something found in books, nor any place external. Wisdom is choosing to think, speak, and do those things which are good so that others teach unto you all their ways freely.

324. Let he who seeks wisdom open his palm. Let her who seeks peace want not. Let those who seek joy give.

325. The fear of the Lord is to love thyself. To love thyself is to love others. Whoever loves himself knows no contention, and wherever contention be not, neither be striving… and this is knowledge.

326. When I have seen the whole of me in my mind's eye, I will set out to realize it by my hands. Once I have fashioned myself by my strength, I will return to think like a child again.

327. Is man not a nut?... Shed thy shell and live sweetly!

328. Let men sow and reap in the earth that others may be filled and refreshed. Everything else leadeth to and sprouts from war.

329. The mind of obedience rests atop feet girded in shoes of humility, peace and love.

330. Blessed is a man whose common sense leads him to educate himself.

331. If you seek victory do not contend with the world in the things they gratify, for those things, they also produce.

332. The purpose of every man is to focus his eyes deep within the darkness of his own heart. And when his eyes have led his feet to the center of his dark soul, let him declare from within, "Let there be light!"

333. When a man decides that wickedness, rudeness, and disrespect on the lips of his inner voice is no longer acceptable and chooses to address himself in a manner of gracefulness, then comments of burden will seek to enslave him from outside himself. When a man decides to learn himself as a student to the evils around him and yet accepting nothing of its fruit inside of him except for the way to avoid them, then the man shall be renowned as a gentleman.

334. Whenever you embark upon new waters seek out those with ships contently set for sail.

335. Let the man of purpose waste not his energies.

336. We are gods because God said so!

337. One should never say those things unto himself that he wishes others not to speak to him.

338. If God be the spirit, and Lucifer the cherub that covers—be it, the flesh, how can man love the things of this world and live, for surely this world is passing.

339. What is the tree of the knowledge of good and evil except an illusion that captured the mind of man. True knowledge is love, and in love good and evil are one and none.

340. When I overcome myself then I shall know God.

341. A man of power is a precious preserver of all of his energy, though he expels it all.

342. God gives unto the giver over the asker.

343. Whatever habits a man holds shall tell the stories of all that liberates or binds him in bondage.

344. Let a man judgeth not strangers, nor those in his neighbor's house. Let a man judge only those in his own fold who are under his own authority.

345. To those who strive for greatness let gentle silence be the first victory.

346. Whatever a woman asketh of God, let her give unto others, that she receives from God what she asks.

347. Whoever reaches for the sun should prostrate themselves below the sandals of the lowest man.

348. Whatever you choose to do, do in the anointing of God; as Christ!

349. Of all those men desire, where shall they lead him except in the way of vanity? But to truth, there is a path of silence and solitude, and here sorrow and compassion dresseth thee for the task of carrying love to the world.

350. To be at peace with the world in all its chaos of good and evil, let a man wage a continuous war against himself alone.

351. Are not the heavens and the earth, the trees and the herbs, the animals and the bushes but places of abode to the servants of God and man? And man alone the temple of God who created all things?

352. We shall all have our days to teach, just as our days to learn. Teach then those below you and learn from those above. Own nothing that you receive for the wise man is surely a steward only.

353. Teach a man not according to how he learns, but according to how he teaches.

354. To know and control thyself is to have the whole universe and all its workings at your command.

355. Pressure will ferment or break according to whether one surrenders or resists.

356. Those who do not righteousness live not but die!

357. Whoever gathers to give all except his own necessity shall live at peace with all men.

358. Chaos!; be it only a straining for order.

359. Until a man stands alone… power he knows not!

360. Let her who desires to be great be great at small things.

361. Dear man, know that the flesh is only clothing and that you are in the flesh. Get then wisdom and instruction so that you may never be over nor under dressed.

362. Why do you ask for repentance with the lips whenever it is for the taking by thy feet and hands?

363. A friend is whoever in their own conduct nurtures one's vision of another when the thing be good.

364. Who once he has found the truth will contend with another over truth but one who deceives himself, thus showing by truth that he is a fool.

365. Let thy prayers unto the Father be thy acts unto men so that you reside in the favor of all.

366. Let whoever considers the morrow not waste today, for if the morrow be in another skin after the shedding off of the present, all that one takes unto himself now will bear fruit later. Let man master his passions and educate today for tomorrow's blessing… Above all, blessed is he who today does good toward his neighbor.

367. I have journeyed in this body for such and such a time, yet I am from eternity to eternity.

368. Truth is not in the find, but rather in the asking, knocking, and in the searching, for who can interpret a thing he has not labored for?

369. Until one can understand the things which are not, he shall not understand those things which are because truth is hidden from him in plain sight.

370. Truth is never known… it simply IS!

371. Let man so reason that he might be pure at last.

372. Whoever seeks out competition has already failed.

373. Who is the master but he who has learned to be simple in all manner of life; simple in thought, simple in word, simple in deed, for in complexity is much worry and little control, until all the parts move as one piece.

374. Shall mankind evolve themselves into the state of the ant and bee? These being together as a unit governed by a queen who nurtures with love and eternal virtue have elevated in thought and joined themselves together in unison for the prosperity of all. What wisdom lies herein!

375. Principles or details? By which to live is the choice of every man. One is without the other while the other embodies the one.

376. Life is only to think, speak and do what is good for others more than for self with joy, peace, and love.

377. Let her who has will-trouble, work out her weaknesses.

378. When I have conquered self, I shall be crowned and hailed as conqueror of the universe.

379. When, through obedience to the law of thy heart, one has come to know love, he shall also become and know truth, for the two are one and eternal.

380. God, I am proud of you! Though I am only a man, when I consider the beast that I was, I stand evermore erect in who I am, for now is eternal and as a man I am made in your own image and likeness… God, I am proud of you!

381. Let her who seeks truth put on all things until none fit.

382. Unto the gentleman doing his duty, being righteous and upstanding in every affair is both his work and his pleasure.

383. Let reason and faith tread together in the pursuit of truth.

384. Let a man so build himself as to weather every storm. If he be moved by anything, in that direction he should fortify himself.

385. Let the true man of greatness never forsake gathering unto himself in solitude and giving of himself where men are gathered. Everything that empties must be filled, and whatever fills must be poured out, because life is in the flowing and never in the stagnation.

386. Many men are learned by the gathering and investigating of information, but few are known wise by the insight of knowledge. Information comes through the channels of the senses, but knowledge through the cavity of the heart.

387. Never allow people to occupy more space than they cultivate.

388. If a man hates his neighbor, he cannot love himself.

389. What good is it to look and see where a man comes from if you do not inquire on where he is traveling?

390. Before I reveal to my enemy my weakness, I shall first by silence force him to reveal every weapon in his arsenal.

391. Until man learns the wisdom of silence, he remains unlearned.

392. The whole world is ever in need of the thorough man.

393. Though a man speaketh the truth a thousand sermons, he has failed to teach even once till he become the truth in his steps.

394. The master and the student are a constant dying and being again born.

395. To think is chaos, but to know is to be still.

396. Whatever you plant should render fruit that nourishes others with life.

397. I pray with the duty of my effort that the Lord might bless the fruit that I bear.

398. Life is to live, death is to die, and man is only attracted to himself.

399. If you never do something different, you'll never be different. Character is the reward of those who explore.

400. Shall a man ever receive by ear words by another that he himself did not whisper within his own heart toward another?

401. If a man is blessed, let him run and pour out himself into others with joy. By this he shall discover that it is impossible to empty, for unto he who gives more shall be given.

402. When a man has his views challenged, let him listen and be thankful because wisdom wishes to teach him something new.

403. Anyone desiring to overcome the world should abide by the law.

404. I appreciate all of today's effort and information because I hold no regrets on yesterday… I've learned to just move on.

405. A man, whoever he is, shall only survive by what he knows.

406. To the teacher the student asks, "What like is life?" and unto the student the teacher replies, "Like me and you!" for in all things as one but separate are cause and effect!

407. THINK NOT GOOD OR BAD, NOR RIGHT OR WRONG, BUT ALONE… JUST!

408. Unless one reaches the end of preparation, the beginning of victory cannot be had. Life only gets better for those who choose to live thankfully.

409. Emotions don't tell you which road to travel, but rather how the weather is where you are, so you know how to dress for the journey.

410. I wish not for conversation where complaints are. I choose to be thankful, so I have nothing to complain about.

411. Question!... Without it a man has no truth, no knowledge, no wisdom, and no understanding, but he who dares to question possesses all of these and reigns with authority. Only unto him will things be laid open and clear.

412. Consider the fruits and their roots because all things have a return, and though blessings may be given unto another, consequences cannot be avoided.

413. Not preparing for tomorrow says, "I wasted yesterday!"

414. Looking down the road causes my feet to step with purpose.

415. In a capitalistic world, the only real education is business and economics.

416. Options are revealed to those who question but given to those who are curious.

417. I shall value the return of activity over the return of experience. Experience I have to wait for, but activity I can enjoy now while investing its return in experience.

418. I'm a leader because I see tomorrow in today.

419. What path to take depends on what I think. Whether I should run or walk is decided by how I feel.

420. Waiting on the perfect moment keeps the moments imperfect. Moving on the imperfect moments gives the sense to know that perfection is better defined "in motion!"

421. To do something great you've got to step out from where you are, turn around and face the crowd so you can see where you've come from and realize the need for service among the proud and the poor.

422. The only way to get out of debt is to get into wealth. Therefore, when I spend, I make sure it grows… I spend my profit's earnings, and all my purchases are reinvestments.

423. Through the struggles of ignorance, I've come to know that if I strive and do well in one area of living, I have done well in them all because through perfecting the one I shall see how to perfect the others.

424. Business is business to those who know the game, but a job or unemployment to those who don't.

425. Confused is the sluggish man… If you want to find confidence, then look for work!

426. Beliefs are built on rumors and hearsays, but understanding is found in experiences.

427. To perceive the end of the morrow today requires that I consider today in yesterday's plans.

428. To the question, "What is life?" I shall answer, "It is about where we are going and how we are going to get there."

429. A man's wealth, whether he be rich or poor, is exposed by the ways of his feet and tongue.

430. Who is it that would be such a fool as to gratify the flesh at the expense of the soul? Woe I say unto you! That which puts on flesh in the womb shall in another, take it off.

431. The death of fear comes by knowledge and understanding.

432. Preparation! To plan to live is to die alive!

433. To the successful… "Never think money, only ponder service."

434. Whoever clouds her soul full of distractions shall never see herself.

435. Truth be that portion in every being that weighs the difference between right and wrong.

436. Those who know that man is always in need of God's favor should never pass on an opportunity to forgive a transgression.

437. Is he who kicks against the gods of any system not but ignorant of the workings by experience, and of the rewards and sacrifices of that system?

438. Excuses belong to the sleeping man.

439. If time is my opponent, let me make the most of it from moment to moment.

440. Whoever is controlled by his own mind is likewise subject to the minds of others.

441. Both failure and success are rewards, but only one is an achievement.

442. I shall claim the status of Mastermind only because my mind has been surrendered to puppetry by the spirit of God.

443. A man of maturity should first be known for wisdom, discipline, and peace.

444. Let not those awake ponder sleep for only the dead worry themselves with inactivity.

445. To him who the universe yields not a chance is crowned a creator of opportunity.

446. Those who do not master their own minds remain slaves to circumstances.

447. The value of any product and service is measured by its rate of circulation.

448. Whenever met with restriction and opposition in any area of pursuit I shall investigate the presentation of the problem itself, and from this I shall birth a new service to combat that which has stood in my way.

449. Only those who dare to strive; who dare to cultivate, who dare to question and demand answers, and never settle for less. ...Those who crown themselves are fit to rule as Kings and Queens.

450. In all the ways of man I shall only be moved by humility, for this be the only thing man cannot pretend.

451. Those things which one speaks and accepts from the lips of others become bondage or freedom, according to the contents of the words.

452. To fear is to be cursed and crushed. Not to fear is to cause the entire universe to render forth its blessings.

453. When a man is searching, he cultivates and plants, taking from sources outside, into himself by way of his five senses. When a man has become, he bears fruit and prunes, giving from the source inside of himself. Here, the contents of the spirit are manifested through the five senses.

454. If a person appeals not to thy friendship for thy own benefit and pleasure through service, obligation cloaked within selfish means shall surely be his intention.

455. All things solid should remain in a cohesive, cooperative state of motion, lest in stillness it should disassemble itself.

456. Appreciation is fleeting to those who wait for its reward, for it is a thing one must create, and this by consistently going the extra mile.

457. To arrive, to know, to truly reach the heights of enlightenment is to be joyously content beneath everyone else.

458. Whatever a man thought of himself at yesterday's close, he shall be at today's opening.

459. Selfish means will always end in solitude because they began with only self in mind.

460. The nature of a man shall reveal the direction of his mind in any situation, even before the formation of the thought.

461. If my heart is against my brother, my smile shall reward my hands with a treasure of gravel.

462. A train will only travel as far as the labor of the one who constructed the track.

463. Why speculate when sureties are all around you!

464. Be blinded not by the labor of a man, for his heart is revealed in his leisure.

465. Be careful to mind thy tongue dear lad, because all that thou sayeth in the seen awaits thee in the invisible and is indeed now active for and against thee.

466. I shall not only think about what I think about, but as well those things that enter my mind to present themselves as thought.

467. If by becoming awake I shall be purposed with a blessing to give unto the world of those asleep… ignorance shall reward me my just due!

468. If I know what you want, then I know how to give you what I want you to have.

469. Increase is the result of effort put forth in gaining reward in any arena in which effort has gained a reward, therefore it is never free but is the further spoils of further efforts.

470. Any man who can move the eyes of another man ought to be praised, for adoration is the façade of love, and envy is a costly gift of any class.

471. As long as a man, having his feet pointed in my direction, holds a sword he shall always see a brick wall.

472. The faster an object moves, the stiller it becomes. The quicker the mind, the calmer the body.

473. Every opportunity that a man misuses there is an even greater opportunity missed.

474. When a man knows how to save, he knows when to give. When a man knows how to give, he knows when to spend.

475. Whenever I am urged to do a thing that is good, I shall strive to do it and to do it promptly lest someone known or unknown be prolonged in receiving their prayer answered, and my own go unheard.

476. Whatever seems troublesome, consider it in relation to what you absolutely need.

477. Because God is God, He will only allow a man to succeed as far as that man has prepared himself for that success.

478. Does a man profess to be wise? …Let him not complain! Does a man profess to have understanding? …Let him not blame others! Does a man profess to have knowledge? …Let no boasting be found on his lips! …Does a man profess to have instruction? …Let him not whine! And for all this he shall be thankful and thanked!

479. He who is isolated has cut himself off from the need and the aid of the world.

480. Be mindful of how you bid your time because every tomorrow is built on today.

481. A master is so because he, with diligence, is a student of students.

482. The one who has a loose tongue is easily controlled and always a slave to his gossips.

483. Many words, words within, and upon words are a sign of a deceitful and oppressive nation.

484. It is better even for the fool to be quiet and enjoy what he enjoys than to open his mouth with transgression and cause his own house to fall.

485. Why should you strain at the task of love… Is it not easier to release the grasp than to break the rod of ego?

486. The thoughts are like screams to him who has learned to properly observe, to correctly see and hear, by the fear of the Lord… Woe unto the hearts of man!

487. Never let chaos go to waste because in every storm lies the opportunity to organize thy steps in stealth.

488. If your growth is an accident and not planned, then you are accidentally planning to fail.

489. When street smarts and common-sense fail, you've got to pick up a book… Education is where observation should lead you!

490. If it were revealed unto man that he was his own judge according to all that he thought, said, and done according to the convictions of his own heart, what then would be his way?

491. All possibilities and all opportunities become apparent, grow and expand with knowledge that one chooses to receive and act upon.

492. I shall search no longer for the clear path because I must make my own way.

493. When I consider all that I have been through thus far, all I wish is that I shall die so that I can start anew, and this with the remembrance of yesterday.

494. By simple understanding I shall strive to turn information into knowledge; knowledge into power, power into wisdom, and wisdom into influence through putting it all to work to serve others.

495. If our bodies be living temples, I would hope that the God of creation lives there.

496. Mastery of anything is nothing more than one mastering self by the exercising of a specific thing and the desire thereof.

497. Let whoever is in search of the philosopher's stone find himself in a library. It is there that men and women have turned whatever it was that they managed to gather into a heap of gold and made themselves into persons of value.

498. The eyes that see the furthest are those who focus on the relations of things to and from other things.

499. Blessed is the man who fears God and knows himself, for by self-governship a man shall stand atop of time.

500. Let all of a man's strivings be in the searching and working out one's life task because after all the vanity done under the sun, only masters shall enter the gates of heaven's kingdom.

501. To gain knowledge is the ability to evolve with intelligence, to grow with honor and dignity, and to mature with respect and virtue. "To have knowledge is to die full and live empty!"

502. I have determined that I shall live in a way that my lifestyle testifies for me and against my accusers on the day of judgment.

503. By much toil in tribulation, by much pain and hurt in the envy and hatred of my enemies, by much sorrow in the pursuit of knowledge, and by much understanding and instruction in facing my own sins, I have learned this… "Despite the thorns and thistles of the night, and the day, whatever it is that you stand for, whatever it is that you believe and engage… for all men be a good example."

504. Fear of anything is dissipated in the knowledge of that thing.

505. Power goes to those who know, yet authority is a gift to those who do.

506. Where responsibility is denied and evaded, dung rolls downhill.

507. Influence is about evolving from a sheep to a shepherd and leading people in a direction that you want them to go for reasons that sprout from within themselves.

508. The greatest measure of success comes when a man has made himself teachable.

509. God works in mysterious ways, but it's up to you to bring His attributes out of people by encouraging goodness in others and praising people for acts of kindness and love and by, most of all, being an example of instruction in these things with your lifestyle in every manner.

510. Better that the things you desire be earned by your own labor than to be the spoils of deceit and treachery because whatever you have by ill-gain will become the booty of a con greater than you.

511. Whoever requires incentives to accomplish a thing will die a loser, for a lack of faith.

512. To walk as a leader… obligation is an opportunity! One must continue to ask oneself, "Who is in control of my life?" and "How can I make a difference for others in a positive way?"

513. Life is wonderfully good no matter what when lived positively on purpose.

514. The world is a beautiful place when you learn how to live.

515. The tallest blade of grass is the first to be cut, and the first to grow back.

516. The man who spends all his time in reminiscent ponder has failed to prepare the day before because today he spends thinking backwards.

517. Better the man to enter a thing prepared than to enter a thing having to prepare.

518. A man who talks in circles, walks in circles, going mad and getting nowhere!

519. Vision is seeing things from other angles and all the way through from where you're standing.

520. You can't break or remake the rules until you learn why and how to obey them. Anything else is the rules breaking you.

521. Just because God said that He was the same yesterday, today and forevermore doesn't mean that He's only one way.

522. Perfection is the ability to make mistakes and learn from them while continuously moving to a better place and blessing others as you go.

523. Though great minds think alike, they do not all think in the same directions.

524. A good leader is measured not by "now" alone, but by "where and why."

525. Let your knowledge be for goodness' sake and your goodness be well cultivated with valuable know and know-how.

526. Without permission, the right thing becomes the greatest transgression of all.

527. Only the people that change the world read, and the things they read are life changing.

528. A true alpha is always in preparation and working something that he has put his mind to. Though he may not always be the alpha, he is nevertheless always an alpha.

529. What one does not live, one should not speak.

530. The secret of life and death and all things in relation and correlation to another, both big and small, left and right, good and evil, God and man, is to never separate anything! It is wise to keep and do things in their proper seasons and in moderation, yet foolish to separate one thing from another. Where a house is divided against itself it falls, yet to perceive all things as a seamless whole is to stand always and firm.

531. Without understanding, common sense is useless!

532. Until you decide where you are going and who it is that you are, you don't know what you don't need nor who it is that you are not.

533. Whenever someone shows you their pride and gives you their attitude, show them your vulnerability and give them humility.

534. Remember this! …"Life goes on, and people are continually being made… and that, to perfection!"

535. To recognize God in others and to seize it is to expose God in you.

536. It is better not to know than to know and not do, for much suffering comes to those who lack labor.

537. Where a person has stopped making decisions, a broken will is sure to follow.

538. I shall only be the fruit that I desire!

539. As it is without, so is it within!

540. Responsibility lies in the necessity.

541. Common sense belongs to everybody, but good sense is the reward of the MAN!

542. Suffering comes to those who know not how to manage themselves according to circumstances.

543. Forgiveness is unconditional love in motion.

544. To truly live is to be as God, who is as we truly are. And that is as no-thing.

545. Through the storm is the shortest path to peace, for without knowing the storm, peace cannot be understood.

546. To be someone and some thing is temporary because birth and death are the cycle of identity, but to be no one or thing is eternal and truth.

547. Gravity is a law subjecting thing because identity has weight, yet to be no-thing is to fly and levitate… Emptiness ascends!

548. To know thyself, the universe, and the gods is to perceive that all is nothing.

549. Being nobody is free and refreshing. It doesn't need constant maintenance like being somebody.

550. To love and serve God is to love and serve all peoples and all things that exist, for nothing that exists outside of He and all things are servants to the whole and His parts.

551. Want not for heaven or hell. Only be where you are now with goodness.

552. To be a son of honor, a man must discipline and conduct himself after the ways of the almighty Father.

553. Should I respect he who gives me what I want above Him who gives me all that I need?

554. Why wait? …pray and work.

555. When the striving has not been striven, the power has not been given.

556. No one can truly repent except he who has peace in mind, and wisdom.

557. Growing up doesn't just happen, it takes effort.

558. To feed your heart, intellect, and body with right and righteous things through the five senses simultaneously with consciousness is to awaken consciously, develop the soul in good health, discipline the body, and renew the mind so that it operates in concordance with the essence.

559. When a person has met their soulmate, the reality is that that person has located, on the physical plane, a desire of the mind that trapped a seed of their own conscious energy from this life or from a life lived that has already passed.

560. Time is the opportunity to perfect the manifestation of the spoken word and thought.

561. When a man seeks to groom a woman to himself, he must exercise the patience and skill of a farmer along with a packet full of seeds.

562. When you change your life, life changes!

563. A woman that a man has to compete for is not good enough for the man.

564. The highest degree of wisdom and knowledge is to forgive because affliction is the path to hating evil.

565. ***It is better to know than to believe, for to believe is to question *** and thus with doubt.

566. In the game of life, it is an impossibility to win for those who seek competition.

567. Abundance is realized as one's own when one loves their neighbor as themselves because it is through togetherness that each one is free and open to give and receive the same.

568. Laws are rules, regulations, and restrictions to those outside the law, and to them the law renders consequences, but to those who reside within the borders of the law, the law is a shield which is there to protect and guard their freedoms and liberty, and surrenders unto them reward.

569. To possess a thing you must give it, to know a thing you must teach it, to teach and give a thing you must be it.

570. Common sense is cheap, but good sense costs much indeed!

571. To know what a man is, observe carefully what he gives.

572. In everyone that I meet I have always and only met myself.

573. When you're smart, you know how stupid you are.

574. In a world full of escalating chaos, the way to control one's environment is by controlling oneself. Only then is the world ever attentive to such a one… his every gesture and action is captured, and his every word becomes law.

575. A man who requires of his own tongue, hands, and mind only the good fruit in which he has ingested has learned righteousness.

576. Common sense is to be measured by the direction that a body of people are headed in, and upon the information by which they operate.

577. An insightful man learns from his own labors, but a discerning man learns from the lessons of others.

578. Being! …comes through conscious action.

579. You will start hearing when you start listening with the purpose to hear, just as you will stop hearing when you stop listening with the will to admit that you do not know.

580. LESS, WITH UNDIVIDED ATTENTION, IS MORE WITHOUT THE HEADACHE OF BEING TOO MUCH.

581. What makes someone smart isn't just what they know, but also the fact that they know something…and it works!

582. The only ones with problems are the people who won't try to solve them. The rest of us only face challenges.

583. Division is a separation of opposition without a common goal. Separation is a dividing of a thing into two or more parts of the whole, working themselves individually and together in a unified cause.

584. To understand this life is to know that cause and effect are only and always one and the same. The effect of one cause is itself the cause of another effect, yet to what end and degree the pendulum swings depends on how you respond and/or react and the temperament of your heart.

585. War is the way to death. The only way to peace is to love and charity.

586. Standing on top of the mountain means learning to move with things rather than against them.

587. If opportunity truly exists, then I must create it or at least create the circumstances from which it arises so that I can seize and direct it as its master.

588. You'll never stop doing that which you continue to entertain.

589. Where slaves react, masters respond.

590. People who compromise with themselves are people who stumble by continually stepping on their own feet.

591. A "want to do" never got anything done!

592. Thinking about life after death is a waste. Just live for now with death in mind!

593. Want a voice? …Quit quoting others and consider things and how to express them for yourself.

594. If you want to be rich, find out what the rich know and do what they do.

595. I would rather evolve in all my moments than to revolt in one.

596. Change is a shock while evolution is soothing… I'd rather just evolve.

597. Life is only lived in one direction. Everything else is a division that leads only to death.

598. If you want to get somewhere and do something, plan it!

599. One need not be afraid of the consequences of doing the wrong thing, but rather made aware of the rewards for doing what's right.

600. The way to experiencing things and growing old well-defined is setting goals and striving to accomplish them.

601. Enough with problems and solutions! Just focus on how to be of service and assistance for a good cause.

602. Breakthroughs are only available to those who consistently chip away at the rock.

603. I don't manage people, I manage duties, and teach people to manage themselves.

604. When I see genuine vulnerability in people it makes me want to climb mountains for them.

605. The secret to staying young is to enjoy growing old.

606. To live life awake is the end of selling dreams.

607. In what you do…just run!

608. If you want to see more, learn to use the eyes of others.

609. Why suffer and struggle with regret when I can grow stronger and conquer with redo.

610. Freedom means everyday labor.

611. The way of no competition is the path of constant victory.

612. Concerning the way and its passage, many consume but few circulate and digest!

613. Why should you fear what you don't know when it's what you don't know?

614. Success is nothing more than fulfilling the responsibility of loving oneself through loving others.

615. To master oneself is the most toilsome thing to do in life, yet never needs to be done, and is the only purpose in life.

616. Book knowledge increases one's effectiveness and efficiency in a time-saving fashion.

617. It takes months to create a habit, every day to keep it consistent, and only one moment to break it.

618. The truth of the mystery is that your whole life awaits you on the other side of this existence where one dreams. Whatever you choose, life or death, it shall be for eternity. Here is only the choice to live or to die.

619. Whenever you have taken in a seed into one of the five gates, whether thou be internally heaven or hell, let quietness and stillness follow until such a seed dies, is born a twig, matures into a tree, and bears fruit so that you do not lose its lesson nor the way of wisdom.

620. The end of fear is where emptiness begins.

621. When one gives up speech, he shall gain an ear. When one gives up sight, he shall gain presence. When one gives up thoughts, he shall be given the way.

622. Still eyes catch even the wind, while those in motion miss even the steps taken by their own feet.

623. The way of discipline is no discipline. By making discipline the law, constant and spontaneous, there are no borders and no regulations… There is only freedom.

624. Strength is found in numbers only where the ignorant contend with persons more ignorant than they. There are some who singularly defeat whole mobs by not contending, but rather by serving or by some other means. These know that authority and its victory are rewarded to those who know how to be free and use all that nature provides as complements.

625. When you obey the law, it doesn't exist!

626. The more consistent you are, the more automatic and instant things become.

627. The difference between motivation and influence is that motivation sprouts from within and only moves toward what is universally right, while influence comes from without and can steer one in the way of right or wrong.

628. Focus is the only lesson in life, while love is the only commandment.

629. To those who hold the philosopher's stone, life is never-ending and eternal. They shall always remain through the minds in which they inhabit.

630. To say that one thing is better than another or that one thing is good and that another is bad is a revelation that a thorn or plank is in thy own eye because you have failed to see things each in their own place. May judgment be only concerning what I do and do not accept for me in this moment.

631. Whatever you decide to do, be steady and determined. Lose your mind and let the task guide you in the way of becoming until you, the task, and the produce are three portions of one whole.

632. When you see a man begging, bless him and encourage him to work so that his soul be not filled with shame. When you see a beggared who cannot work, bless him double so that he may bless another who can work and thus be relieved of his torture and misery.

633. If you are not building yourself, then you are either destroying yourself or wasting away… there are only two directions.

634. There is no mesmerization in familiarization!

635. An ever-increasing circle of knowledge and experience, plus a manageable circle of well-cultivated friends, equals phenomenal success.

636. If there were no clocks, everyone would always be on time.

637. Exposure is the manifestation of selfishness. Revelation is the coming of truth.

638. Truth is found in one's wholeful usefulness to the needs of others.

639. Correct vision comes with correct positioning.

640. In a world of left and right; high and low; good and bad; back and forward; we and them; success and despair, the feet that are secured in gray shoes shall tread the most ground because they have equal passage through the valleys and atop the hills with just enough repose and poise to avoid extremes. Where extreme begins, contentment is destroyed, and want is born, and this is to suffer.

641. Unusefulness and misuse are simply imperfection!

642. One cannot destroy what one does not know.

643. To die enlightened is to live immortal, to die a fool is to have never existed.

644. He who is not responsible with wisdom is born a fool.

645. A man who seeks ideas should ask questions.

646. Knowledge is death to a man who fails to use it.

647. When a man controls himself, he controls the world in relation to him.

648. A man who is experienced in everything that he knows is a smart fool for failing to learn from others.

649. In all of man's searching to understand, in all his toiling and striving to earn wisdom, in all of his trials and struggles to gain knowledge, this he should know… That sometimes storms arise not because of his past transgressions but because of his coming triumphs. The hand of God which is ever reaching down into the world is only met by those who dare to reach up.

650. Woe to the fool who blesses not himself with kindness and humility unto others while it is yet today. Knoweth he not that all that is now is the effects of yesterday, and the causes of tomorrow?

651. If a man understands his power, thus knowing that he has in him the freedom to choose his every cause, and yet remains powerless to choose the effects therefrom, let such a one ever strives to choose for himself, in every occasion that which is good and honorable so that he never be dishonored, and always stand upright upon the earth.

652. I can!

653. Excuse yourself from complaints by only asking questions when looking for answers.

654. If you fail to pay attention to the details for your own betterment, someone else will pay attention to them for your downfall.

655. To make a dream a reality, you have to prepare to bear its fruit.

656. With the earth and all of its seasons, the way to a better world is by each man improving himself.

657. From moment to moment, that which is unknown is certain and all that there is.

658. Heavy is my burden, and yet light is my heart, for though evil be on every side, You are near. With one hand You press down on me, and with the other You hold me up that I might know You in my inner-man.

659. Whenever one lowly has decided to climb the mountain of knowledge that he may become wise and commune with the eternal Father, and by doing so, ever mark his light in the heavens, he shall surely then by the Father's abounding grace face the effects of his low man's wretched ways. If then he can conquer the forces of his own karma, he shall surely stand atop the peak of life crowned with understanding and know the mercy of God.

660. All things are only ever exactly what you say they are!

661. The only way to truly know someone else is to truly reveal oneself.

662. When I look at me, I see you, but when I look at you unaware of myself, I miss everything.

663. The empty hand is the most valuable and cherished of all because it has a multitude of uses.

664. All words of power are and have only ever been vocal expressions well-lived, and therefore shall only be authorized by those who dare to experience their joy and their sting.

665. The whole purpose of life and living is to enjoy all things, and yet to choose God above every sensation.

666. If every day you smile at everyone you see, you shall never go a day without receiving a smile.

667. Hard and happy labor gives steadiness to your hands, light and stillness to your eyes, and understanding and instruction to your mind.

668. You can always know what a man will accept by what he approves of himself.

669. You live how you define things!

670. Better to be bothered because you are rich than to be ignored for being poor.

671. Do not fear more the man who loves to win, nor he who hates to lose, but above all fear him to whom winning and losing matters not, for he is absolute and at once the most dangerous and noble man in the kingdom.

672. Before the cut of the sword, let the pen bleed out.

673. I have thought… not to think!

674. Let a man only take as much rest as he gives activity; as much food as water; and as much standing as sitting, that in all things he may be balanced.

675. The key factor in the mastery of things, and that of self, is thus… Things, being themselves external, have their end points, yet the I is endless and eternal. It is a thing and not, and like the rungs on a ladder, still.

676. Things will be what they will be and what they will be is what they are.

677. What if the thorns of a rose were all the previous attempts to blossom that failed before the blossoming became!

678. The difference between two feet equal in stride, where one leaves its owner exhausted and the other fills its owner with vibrance is that the first is hurried and concerning while the latter is well-paced and thoroughly enjoyed.

679. There are two types of artists but only one type of experiencing art as an expression. The former are those persons in love with galleries and collecting works for observation, and the latter are those people responsible for the strokes of the brush and the sculpting of the clay.

680. Think good of others, and you must be done good by others.

681. Justice is the act of doing yourself and others good by God's standard.

682. A man who conducts himself and his affairs according to another's perspective is a slave twice.

683. What have a dead man but no thing, and having no thing, he is fully alive.

684. Lose thyself not in appearances nor in the creation thereof but let everything that you do be thoroughly done.

685. There is always room for one who makes good use of what he has.

686. To move with the course of change is the door to expressing individuality.

687. Don't be concerned with fish until you can catch one.

688. To capture and express through oneself the whole world in a moment is to rise as the spokesman of creation itself.

689. As a rule of life: Whenever you meet resistance; when you're doing the wrong thing, then you know that you're going the wrong way.

690. There is nothing worse than a man who oppresses himself with the illusive joys of ignorance.

691. One's only importance lies in his ability to freely serve others.

692. A true master never tries to impress his will upon others because he knows that every man must find himself for himself, and within himself only.

693. If one can never be greater, but only as good as his master, be sure that those whom you choose to follow along your path have surmounted every fear and obstacle with which you struggle.

694. To truly know what is and is not; to become rather than to know, make sure that what goes in the head exits the pores of one's whole body rather than leaking from the tongue.

695. To become whatever I will to do, is the height of understanding.

696. What is useful is whatever directs me to me.

697. Truth is in the do, not in the undone.

698. Those who conquer fear discuss possibilities no more.

699. Through detachment, focus is specified.

700. Sometimes you've got to do things a little different to see yourself in a new way.

701. Only he who can answer the five Ws and the H can say that he knows a thing.

702. Inside of oneself is the only ground where the seed of success can be planted. Others taste of its fruit and desire a harvest in themselves.

703. If a man has not built himself by the methods in which he requires of others he cannot lead others by those methods.

704. To live what is written to the letter is truth.

705. It is the gift of God that mankind is able to apply themselves in the labor of knowledge and grow wise with understanding, and thus honor Him by service and council to the ignorant in the world, that by doing so they may die a lovely death rather than the death of ignorance with which they so rebellantly inflicted themselves.

706. When you focus your full attention on something you are getting to know yourself because you are acting with self-awareness.

707. If you spend all of your energy in defending yourself, you'll come to realize in the pit of your failure that you were only holding yourself back.

708. Broken people are the most beautiful of all.

709. Whoever you are, whatever you are… be a success story!

710. It's not what "I think," it's only what "it is" … Things will explain themselves!

711. Simply be who and what you are, and remember, you can always add and take away.

712. Only a fool rushes with possessions not his own.

713. Let us affect each other with smiles and let that be the energy that gives each of us the strength and aspiration to carry on and overcome any obstacle that we face.

714. To deal with my own mind is the wisest thing to do.

715. To understand God; to know the Tao… to perceive wisdom, and to find understanding and truth is like the air which carries all things and is itself unseen. It is within and without all things. It gives unto one thing oxygen from another's waste and yet unto this other carbon from the waste of the first. These cannot be sustained upon what they produce, but alike with all things, must depend upon, in equanimity, all other things in a give-and-receive relationship, that all things might be both servant and master unto all others in equal proportion to themselves… and still the air is itself dependent on none but itself, for without all other things it is manifested and not.

716. There is a major difference between the mastery of a thing and that of oneself. Each is to be respected and understood in the differences of, and therefore valued and placed properly. In the journey of the one, the other can be lost, yet in the finding of the other, as a cause, shall render the effectual fruitage of perfecting all things in which the mind and body shall be given to do.

717. Let man give up his consciousness unto the subconscious and return to instinct his faculty of thought, that he may rejoin in balance with every other thing, and maintain his place in holding intuitively, in moderation to all things, himself.

718. A man that minds his own can make it alone!

719. Why would I hit the bottom and not strive for the top?

720. Love is free when you accept it! To accept is to surrender!

721. Street smart means you can survive on the bottom. Book smart means you can survive on the top.

722. Two people sitting doing nothing… One never did anything, and the other is only taking a break. Decide who you want to be!

723. The height of life is to simply release and enjoy living.

724. When you can see the future that you labor for, why worry about now!

725. If your worst will not drive you to do good, your best shall surely destroy you.

726. He who takes is never ready to receive!

727. It is impossible to understand a thing in which one does not know, and yet it is impossible to know a thing that one has not become.

728. Forget birth and death and you will learn to live!

729. I shall not label myself so as not to cut off, nor overextend, the force's power to work through me good or bad, but rather I shall only reply: "If that is how I seem to you, then that is how I seem to you!"

730. Let he who professes to be wise chart his steps, his manner, and his speech upon the silver linings of all extremes that he may draw all to the way and deter none.

731. All things are possible to those who ask, seek, and knock, for those are the ones who will not, nor can they, be denied.

732. At times, one must become a part of the problem to be the solution!

733. Would a wise man argue? …Never!

734. You never know how far you can ascend until you free the depths of your heart of all its weights.

735. Three things will make a man great: Always eat the words of God, always be working in the way of one's inner vision, always remain humble! These three things make man great.

736. Only a good heart and a sober mind can hold the secrets of God.

737. To discern the heart, watch the hand!

738. Never send the wicked to gather the meal, and never send the righteous to take counsel with fools.

739. How you treat other people will determine how great you live!

740. When the weeds arise in the place where you have sown good things, worry not, but rejoice because the soil is rich!

741. When there is nothing that you want, everything you gain!

742. If I give all that I understand to be the character of God unconditionally, I shall undoubtedly enter into His kingdom.

743. From the many trials came understanding!

744. Let the one who seeks to be rich pleasure himself with knowledge, having ignorance as his greatest foe. Let the one who strives to be great and revered humble himself, finding for himself joy in the act of giving and service, submitting himself even to the pride and conceit in man, for these evils he must know above all. Let the one who desires faith receive from all with graciousness. Let gratitude be his guide and his way. Let he who seeks to know God and His righteousness consider the seed and how all things produce after their own kind. Let him gaze deep within himself knowing that all things end as they began. Let him know that time is a gift that man may measure and observe the process of life in its expansion, and see that he is the king of God and know that God is enthroned in His kingdom.

    Let the simple question, let the poor serve, let the weak be enriched in wisdom, that the labor of the strong bless the children, and let the great know that all that he has done should be credited to the people, that they may love you when you go down to the grave.

745. Do this & remember Me
    Why in the world would you turn from Me? Did I not shed my blood?
    Did I not stretch my arms, so you could be free?
    Did I not pay the price?... Did they not pierce my side?
    ... So you could be my wife... Do this and remember me!

I could have been as selfish as you are. I could have kept it to myself. Because I knew just what you are, I gave until there was nothing left, I never spoke a word at all, even though they spit on me.
Eli! Eli! Lema sabachthani!... truly this man was a king! Why in the world would you turn from Me?... Did I not shed my blood?
Did I not stretch my arms, so you could be free?
Did I not pay the price?... Did they not pierce my side?... So you could be my wife... Do this and remember Me!
My master washed his hands clean. He couldn't find a reason for you to die. Things are far from what they seem. The crowd is yelling "crucify!"
I'm forced to watch you carry your cross. I think I'm starting to change my mind. We gambled for your robe... Somebody said you were the vine!
* "Father please forgive them, they don't know what they do, but because they hate me now, I commit my spirit to come to you."
Why in the world would you turn from Me?... Did I not shed my blood?
Did I not stretch my arms, so you could be free?
Did I not pay the price?... Did they not pierce my side?... So you could be my wife... Do this and remember Me!
Why do you persecute that righteous man?... He didn't deserve such pain. You're as guilty as I am... Father, I believe in Your name. I am just a filthy rag, but I know You can wash me clean. Please accept me as I am, and wipe away these stains.
* "My dear son, you have been set free. Because you want me now, today in paradise you will reside with Me."

Why in the world would you turn from Me?... Did I not shed my blood?
Did I not stretch my arms, so you could be free?
Did I not pay the price?... Did they not pierce my side?...
So you could be my wife... Do this and remember Me!

746. O' how sweet were the pains of life when the victory came!

747. Let the tears of sorrow shower the mountain top and the praises of joy echo in the bed of the valley.

748. Let all things by Him who is of the Common herd be done without prejudice, and with right reserved!

749. O' wise King! When you are among the people, be of humility and service, and when you are on the throne, noble and ruthless!

750. In all the weight of your toils remember that the hardest ground to bear is the topsoil which lies directly under the shine of the sun.

751. The crowd; they bite, they gossip and mock, they slander, they blame and shout. All is to the glory of the new man in you… Many weeds appear and there is much pruning on the way to the producing of good and ripe fruit… … Say not a word, it is your blessing to endure!

752. For a seed to sprout and rise, it must go against the grain in search of the sun. Now consider the crowd, and do the same!

753. Where the demand closes the door, the question opens it wide… Surely the question shall carry my feet farther!

754. Whatever, wherever, whenever… Study & practice!… study &practice!

755. What good is the willie of a horse who won't gallop the huff, or the roar of the lion that won't hunt or lead? The tongue is powerless without the feet!

756. If common-sense is the mind of those on the bottom, consider better if you desire to rise!

757. The wise man alludes to the way of nature, but he is holy, to the way of the creator.

758. The world, and life itself, shall be hard or soft depending on what each one determines his thought and attitude to be, and whatever each one decides let his own face wear it to his own glory or shame that he may receive his due…" Smile for me!

759. If man can think himself where his body has not been and where his eyes have not seen, what shall we say that man truly is?

760. If you haven't lost yourself in a thing, how can a thing make of you its master?

761. The difference between expectation and surprise… you saw one coming!

762. A half-successful person is a complete failure.

763. A word spoken progresses the thought.

764. Whether or not you value time, time will tell by the revelation of who you become.

765. Won't your steps be ordered if you just plan them first?

766. If you have a desire to grow, have the sense to plant a seed to support it.

767. A fool lets his talking force him to think, but a wise man will cause his thinking to give him the right to speak.

768. By maturity, all things to a man are investments.

769. Information be only either a seed or a weed, and its harvest is measured in what you do with it.

770. That which is a restriction to the poor becomes a privilege to the rich.

771. If time heals, let us hope for plenty of it.

772. The right to anything is alone in the courage to take it.

773. To know the way, let the reward determine the path.

774. Taking shortcuts is the quickest route to nowhere.

775. If I cheat my way to the top, I'll stand before the world as its greatest failure.

776. Did you accomplish something and reward yourself for doing so?... Great! Now get back to work so the spoil doesn't ruin you.

777. Let the farsighted be attained in the near, let the large be mounted in the small.

778. Fundamentals, be it in anything is the seat of understanding.

779. After I have conquered the mountaintop, I shall return to the valley bed because it is there on the bottom where I gain the true wisdom of the climb and the peak of the victory.

780. Children are given things, while adults go and find them.

781. The words of a man of worth shall never fail to outlive him.

782. If my children will be driven by my effort to carry the torch further than me, then let me strive to accomplish all within my potential.

783. When a man begins to think, his pen shall be his greatest ally.

784. Nothing fails to give way when you fail to give up.

785. I suppose that the roaches shall always outlive the rats and the people shall outlive the government.

786. You can't be real with God and fake with people.

787. The condition of a man's house is mirror to his soul.

788. Until you've given everything you haven't the right to complain, but once you've given all, there is no way that you would.

789. To become the super-man is to retain the seed within the vessel until it travels through the sea of the spine spilling over into the crown and forehead where it gives light to the eye and then by the cavities of the heart is mixed with the blood and imprinted in the cells. This is to know and become like God.

790. Two things that are common to all who dare to advance… praise and scorn!

791. Being shown what to do is to be taught but doing what you've been shown to do is to learn.

792. When you consider your current life activities, are you going places?

793. It's never what you have. It's what you think.

794. If you're not larger than your environment, then you're probably in your grave.

795. Nothing ever stays the same. If you're not getting smarter, you're what?

796. The world is unapologizing, and rarely do they forgive, so before you take and give, stop and ask self, "Have I reached deep enough within myself and have I the courage to give all?"

797. Meet uninvited questions with unresolved answers, lest you cast your pearls unto swine.

798. When you strike gold there is no use in searching for silver.

799. When a man is in tune, his way is easy and his sight clear.

800. Being a gossip says you're wasting someone else's time as well as your own.

801. When the scores are all tallied, when the talk is all heard, are you the headline or are you only one of those small guys in the crowd not big enough for a buzz?

802. If we never talk, it's probably because we think different thoughts.

803. What good is being smart without education?

804. Ask whatever question that you will but ask it only of the knowledge from which it arises.

805. That you always rise and are never without honor, be always and only influenced by someone or thing greater than you and aright.

806. Common sense is knowing that you know right from wrong. Good sense is choosing to do right over wrong because of the universal law of karma.

807. Humility is the greatest aspect of confidence.

808. What is life in the scope of good and evil but the up and down, and man between heaven and earth but layer upon layer.

809. I quit trying to figure evil out and decided to just hate it… I traded in sense for wisdom; the fear of the Lord!

810. You can work for money, make money, or create money. The choice is yours!

811. This life boils down to two things: what did you do with time and is it worth eternity?

812. I am more than a man. I am a son of God!

813. The most beautiful thing in the world is a woman who fears the Lord, and the most heinous is a man excelled in childishness.

814. No man can nor shall know truth in the absolute but he who is absolute in his hatred of evil, for this is to love God.

815. Being proud of self only leads to being disappointed in self. Be proud of something greater.

816. If you're not failing and yet not conquering, then you're only surviving and this is worse than both the others.

817. Thought without preparation is not thought at all. It is fantasy. To truly think requires preparation.

818. We were made to live by the wisdom of doing the right thing not by the experience of doing what is wrong.

819. Father, with the complexity in which you made me, I will simply praise You.

820. Legacy! Either you build it or after being misunderstood you'll also be forgotten.

821. Curiosity plus courage equals education.

822. Strength without conditioning is a powerful weakness.

823. By my words have I established immortality.

824. Want to know a man's worth…give him something to talk about…if he can't hold water, he ain't worth a damn!

825. If you try to master wing chun then you can and probably will, yet you limit yourself to the very edge of mastery, but if you use the art and way of wing chun kung-fu to master yourself then there is no limit to the levels you can reach, and maybe you will find the uncharted course and master life.

826. If I strive and so dare to reach for the stars then perhaps my entail will live among them and shine brightly.

827. There is a revolution of some sort in my belly. I can taste its residue in my mouth. I can hear its call deep within my mind. All before me plays a part in its birth, and it keeps me restless in my soul. I have yet to understand its nature and the full of what is required of me but with all of me I do yearn for its full course, for to be common is to choose the nature of man over the likeness of God and I have decided to die in the image of the creator no matter what the cost.

828. I was common and ordinary until I decided too not be so.

829. History is the scribing of today's events for tomorrow's remembrance.

830. The wrong perspective is what anyone thinks and says about me that conflicts with and contradicts what I say of myself and decide to be.

831. My power surpassed that of my enemies when they made me a factor and I chose not to make them the same.

832. A man cannot command a dying nation to live without also being willing to himself bring about its death.

833. How can wisdom teach a man who won't follow the first instruction!

834. Do not let holding your ears to the street cause your head to be buried in the sand.

835. Anything done without character is flawed.

836. True understanding will lead one to himself for all things, even his own faults.

837. When choosing a side consider well the fact that prey are noisy and predators are quiet.

838. When a hunter goes out to hunt of any breed, they are quiet, watchful, cautious, and calculating with acute alertness while the prey are noisy, busy, out of tune and often a part of a crowd…predators set out with goals, but prey go about often without restriction. Considering this who are you?

839. If you've been perfect and never made any mistakes your whole life, how can you really understand the difference between what's wrong and right, especially with the severity of which you judge others?

840. The best things in life don't come at a discount, they require full price.

841. Nothing makes a man more wicked, more heinous, evil, and vile than to be unforgiven and treated according to his sin because in this his shame and his guilt will cause him to fear and to hate with unmerited vengeance.

842. Better than strength and speed is timing and a fingertip feel for the right thing at the right moment. And better than power is authority.

843. Because good and evil has been written good and evil shall come to pass.

844. If I do everything with excellence, should I not find myself among the great? ...Let me not complain then while I am counted with the worthless lest I grow ignorant of the way.

845. Labor and time! Labor and time! ...The absolute of value.

846. Never deny yourself the opportunity to grow. Things that hold no value in this regard will naturally fall away.

847. When I was a student, I looked for the master. When I became a teacher, I realized that the master was the mystery of the word. When I became a master, I was only a student possessing the will and courage to work out the instruction which nature has written before me.

848. Power is best exerted in quietness, and strength is magnified in patience.

849. Patience is the staff of the wise, endurance, the sword of the faithful and temperance is the crown of the king, with justice as its center jewel.

850. If the blacker the berry, the sweeter the juice then beware of the seed of the fruit.

851. The struggle is no longer the focus of the oppressed. It is the will and responsibility to build today with the bricks of every yesterday's battles, despite today's afflictions. "Be strong, be wise, be focused and work out your own salvation!"

852. After looking on the wretched and the noble I have concluded that when a man is extremely dangerous then he is extremely kind.

853. Not enough that you have talent. You must enterprise, lest you be left with an unyielding hobby.

854. Like light, if you move faster than time you will shine. To prepare and plan out the arrangements of the mind is to step before time, and the accomplishment of one's goals causes the face to shine and the feet to move with gracefulness.

855. A thin line lies between gods and men, but a vast gulf between boys and legends.

856. Learn when it's told to you, teach when it's asked of you, and in the in between…pray!

857. When a man respects those he does not know he is trusted by those who know him.

858. To become a student, one must humble himself but to become a teacher one must humble himself twice.

859. When all else fails, you know what doesn't work.

860. When the whole world's eyes are upon you remember that you are standing on higher ground still.

861. If I choose the good the bad will show itself but if I choose the bad the good will surely evade me. The power to choose only remains with the good.

862. When you're moving at the speed of light it can appear as if you're standing still but when you're standing still there is never enough time in the day.

863. A man filled with misery complains. One full of joy blesses. A man grateful gives. Those who take, fear all things. But God and nature only favor the good.

864. If life and death both lie in the power of the tongue, and man by that faculty the ability to bind and to lose in the heavens and in the earth loose then your right to riches and live prosperously.

865. I find that if after I put forth the petition, I keep watch diligently for it's coming to pass that I will actually pray without seizing.

866. Opportunity to a lazy man looks like too much work, to a bitter man, like a burden, to the complaining man, like a problem, to a fragile man, like a hazard, to a cautious man, like a worry. But to a man prepared opportunity appears just as it is… as a ladder and bridge to exactly where they decided to go.

867. Do not believe in the people unless the people believe in God lest your ignorance become a snare unto the land and a vexing on your soul, for a people lives yet persons are soulless, having a liveness in the flesh but being dead in spirit.

868. The worth of a master is measured by the value of his students.

869. When a man is imprisoned and held in bonds it is the darkness and cruelties that lay in the recesses of his own mind, and the evils of mankind in every facet of mankind's nature that he must wrestle with for his freedom. To lose this war is death certain in all of its forms.

870. You can live adjusting to life's changes or you can live making all things adjust to you.

871. When you can tell the truth then you can think straight.

872. The prison cave for me became a mine rather than a grave.

873. Living in yesterday today leaves you no future.

874. The seed of fear causeth a man to bear the fruits of shame, doubt, complaining, blame, worry, lying, blindness, confusion, and judgmentalism.

875. When you have the opportunity to help when things matter greatly to someone else, consider that something of great importance may be about to come upon you.

876. A man stands or falls in whether or not he contradicts himself.

877. Immaturity outside of childhood is possibly the greatest flaw.

878. You're not promised tomorrow, nor are you promised today. The only thing that you are promised is yesterday and it has already passed away.

879. It doesn't take heart to inflict pain on others. It takes heart to endure and to pardon the afflictions of others.

880. If I don't work for you or owe you something, and if I'm not your child nor you mine, don't greet me with questions. Be polite and make sense by greeting me with a simple explanation of who you are and what you want, and by this you may just come to know me.

881. Learning to keep your word and consistently so often begins with not giving it too often.

882. Too many a men worry themselves against the atrocities of history, with finding and knowing the truth when all that is necessary is that they be truth to others. This is nothing more than to be honest in all thy ways.

883. In this journey, above all, miss not the many times that the butterfly escapes the cocoon.

884. When you try to think you prevent yourself from knowing. When you simply know, thinking becomes a natural faculty.

885. Without the slightest knowledge of the length of time allotted, would you not dare to make the most of "these" moments!

886. Give up the senses and the mind shall find you.

887. No paved road can ever be truly mastered by any who travel thereby for its trail and its way has already been blazed and established. By its direction many may find the way to the door leading inside themselves and become masters of mankind and still few may find a thing that is unknown.

888. Greatness resides not at the peak of the mountaintop but at the bottom at the foundation.

889. Energy begets energy, and those who do not labor shall lack the sweetness of sleep.

890. Success demands consistency!

891. If you want peace then quit wanting.

892. By chaos the law is established, but by law chaos is organized.

893. The law brings about the death of chaos and chaos gives birth to the law.

894. If you want to be the boss, then you must run the game with rules.

895. Worth turns to value when potential becomes who you are.

896. Enterprise brings money, knowledge brings power, character brings respect, vision renders inspiration.

897. Gratitude given in the beginning gives way to wisdom and leads to humility, but where it is only given in the end there is much striving, grief, and the pride of life.

898. There is nothing wrong with moving quickly when I am prepared, but to be unprepared and impulsive is self-destructive.

899. All that is required of you from life is that you expand.

900. When we struggle and things aren't going our way, do we continue to try to press? …Learn then, how to accept NO!

901. When the mind's eye wants to see, the spirit must learn to feel because to feel is to become one with everything else at once.

902. Take the game seriously but never the money. The money comes and goes but the game is where we rise or fall.

903. Law and chaos complement each other. Chaos rests in the law but never can the law rest in chaos because it is ever watchful and active.

904. Receive a thing as a task and it shall become a gift to give unto others.

905. Either take time, or rush with all things.

906. Everybody's a genius until things go wrong!

907. The game is not just about how you move, it's about how you live. Character is King!

908. When you have given yourself to a thing it shall in turn give its essence to you and by this you shall become and understand such a thing.

909. Sometimes in order to minimize the risks over time means you have to raise them to enormous rates now.

910. A message to man: "Let God be your weakness and your strength and you shall never fail to stand."

911. If you live dying, you must die living.

912. Let familiarity and similarity be the introduction to change for an easy transition.

913. Life can be messy and men forgetful so in whatever you find to do, clean up as you go!

914. Death by natural or unknown causes says, "We don't want to acknowledge God or the truth that He said so."

915. Let the focus of life be death… If you don't earn it then you deserve it!

916. Death! It's what we did to ourselves so accept it.

917. If you have to steal it, it may be because having it would do you greater harm than not.

918. The man who is untrustworthy has absolutely nothing. No value, no worth, no name, no honor, no respect, no life.

919. Study and study hard. Be thorough in all thy ways, every day seeking to be better than the day before in doing good.

920. The objective of the whole game is to be used and to use; to never cut yourself off from the resources of others and likewise to never deny others right to your own. And do all this with a cheerful heart and a motive to do good for all, for we are all the world over only stewards to what belongs to God alone.

921. Be careful "now" to know the Lord because there is an evil that awaits you on the other side. Light shines bright as the day and what is in the darkness and darkness itself feareth the Lord and are subjected by His word.

922. A lack of preparation is the expressed expectation to fail.

923. Speed is good but timing is better. Where speed can cause one to at times over-extend, over-exert, to strike and reach out beforehand and expend excessive amounts of energy, to be on time is perfect every time.

924. One cannot be free without the full knowledge of his bondage.

925. Choosing the lesser of two evils can still lead you to Hell.

926. Number two isn't just last. It's also the first loser.

927. To receive the favor of God is to be endowed with the favor of all things in His creation. However, in this world, that means to definitely have enemies. Do pray for the courage to face your enemies in the fear of the Lord.

928. Who?... What?... When?... Where?... How?... Are those your first questions? Or do you first ask why? Your first question reveals your position and how you regard yourself.

929. Life's greatest work is bearing children.

930. You never stop being the student unless you reject becoming the teacher.

931. There are worlds and levels to consciousness, so while you are here in this life do build yourself up lest you find yourself in the realms of Hell when you awake on the other side of sleep. This is the mystery of your dreams when you rest.

932. Consistency makes man willing.

933. A smoker's prayer is the remembrance of his glory days.

934. Casting assumptions without a firm base of knowledge leads the heart of man to fear.

935. Relationships take time but love requires eternity.

936. Experiences and their outcomes make us who we are.

937. In all of life what can a master be but one who experiences and expresses fearlessness.

938. Having "no fear" comes from cultivating the ability to foresee the potentialities, and to prepare and settle on doing what it takes to accomplish the best outcome for your own absolute success.

939. Never try to be too good nor too bad in their extremes, but rather understand the center line between the two and acquire the wisdom of both. In the center judgment is null because what one condemns in one moment shall be his path of survival in the next.

940. How did I get here
I remember that old fishin' hole,
And that open field where we used to roam.
Cows moving in the pasture,
Sunday school classes and that fiery pastor.
I remember quail huntin' and skinning a deer,
Picking peas and planting crops every year.
Chasing girls and all the fights, and staring
At stars with my wishes every night.
How did I get here?
City slickin' and chasing women down every road
Where lies become every story told
And after all the dirt weighing on my soul
Whoever knew that I'd be coming home
How did I get here?
I remember swinging an axe and cuttin' grass,
Feeding hogs and fresh grape juice by the glass.
Bluebonnets, honeysuckles and raspberries,
Nana's pancakes with butter and grape jelly.
I remember copperheads and rattlesnakes,
Gravel roads and picket stakes.
That crazy old dog Buster,
Mud pies and that old smokin' Duster.

The Philosopher's Stone

How did I get here?
Broken hearted and penitentiary for many years
Where chasing dreams turned into fears
And after all the tears I shed trying to drown my wrongs
Who ever knew that I'd be coming home
How did I get here?
I remember sheets hanging in the doorway,
No food and all of the dishes I threw away.
Spring cleaning and Sunday dinners,
Hot summers, floods and freezing winters.
I remember Christmas with no gifts to give away,
Pine trees and reading that King James every day.
That old raggedy mailbox,
Chasing the school bus and skippin' rocks.
How did I get here?
From drug use, prostitutes, and breakin' rules
Where all the cool just turned into fools
And daughters that I barely knew would make me
Want to be a man
Who ever knew that I'd be coming home
How did I get here?

941. The objective of knowledge, the path to understanding and the ability to grasp wisdom is in simply trying things out for oneself. In so doing, if it is good for you keep it, but if not discard it. Do not judge anything as good or bad because it may be that you are beyond it or not yet eligible to grasp it. you must try it to the point where by discernment you can perceive whether or not it suits you. If it does not, then go no further.

942. In this life what you collect and become shall surely show in the hereafter. This is only the training ground so be knowledged, wise and built up, yet in Christ you shall overcome.

943. If God divided men because together, we would seek to make for ourselves a name in the heavens, why do we as divided men seek peace? And why when unified do we not cultivate and cherish the earth?

944. The wisdom in being humble is knowing that there is always some force, some being, and someone ever awaiting to render the law whether it be for good or evil. Humility provides the solitude and space to prepare oneself to counter, resist, ward off and even to conquer adversity how, where and when it comes because in our journey through life where lessons make for wisdom, by our mistakes and our strivings, adversity will surely come.

945. The objective is to not only transform but through continuous transformations, to transcend.

946. At this point in the process of my development I am not sure what it will take to pull me back once I have gone so far but I think the greater knowledge is to know how to keep myself from reaching such a point.

Kirk A. Gaither II

Closing

If all that mankind has done and has thought to do; both his failures and his successes have been written, let whoever seeks to contribute something surround himself with the archives of effort and the instruction of "how to." This work is a monument to those who create wealth rather than make it alone, by the plowing of their own soil and the bringing forth and strengthening of their own personal value. In "The Science of Getting Rich" Wallace D. Wattles states, "The very best thing you can do for the world is to make the most of yourself," and again, "The world is advanced only by those who more than fill their present places." Florence Scovel Shinn in her book "The Game of Life and How to Play It" states, "Man only dares use his words for three purposes, to heal, bless or prosper."

Let every man and women who looks here upon this work understand these things through practice. Let each one understand this in respect to the author and what is hoped for you. Who am I?... A man of character, an explorer, a developer, a teacher and student. I am a man who searches for the heart of God and wants the absolute best for all people together. I am a man of many failures, many mistakes, and as well, many lessons. I am a gentleman and an advancing man!

Kirk A. Gaither II

ACKNOWLEDGEMENTS

I'd like to thank CADMUS PUBLISHING for making this possible, and I'd like to thank Albert LaSane for illustrating the cover page.

About the Author

In 2008, Kirk Gaither II was arrested in San Antonio, Texas for felony aggravated kidnapping. At trial in 2010 he received a 25-year prison sentence in the Texas Department of Criminal Justice Detention Center.

During his time in the San Antonio County jail awaiting trial the change that began a month earlier while Kirk was still on the street began to truly unfold. What truly began at the birth of his first daughter "faith," encouraged with the coming of his second "love," was a month prior to being jailed in San Antonio, Texas on felony kidnapping charges brought to full fruition. While in county and throughout his prison term to date, Kirk the man, as a son of God, has been birthed and exercised in the word of God and the passing away of the immature and ignorant man-child has been completed.

"When I was a child, I spoke like a child, I thought like a child, I reasoned like a child. When I became a man, I gave up childish ways," (1 Cor 13:11). This Bible verse stands as a personal testament to the transformation and new life that Kirk has been given. While in prison Kirk redeems the time by making it useful in the way of increasing his usefulness to the world at large and to his peers in his unit community. The unit library serves as a university where Kirk remains to be a faithful visitor, studying a wide range of subjects. Outside of his studies, Kirk trains and teaches in the style of Wing-Chun Kung Fu. Kirk also teaches to other offenders business, law, financial management and planning, astrology, and most of all the word of God. Kirk has ascribed one verse above all others to the many things he has been given in the way of education (mental, spiritual, emotional, and physical wealth). "Seek ye first the kingdom of God and His righteousness and all other things will be added unto you," (KJV, NKJV). It is the author's experience that by following this one verse's instruction you can rise from lost to found, from ignorant to right-squared, from hated to loved, and from rags to riches!

Kirk plans on opening several business ventures after he is released from prison, and even while he remains to be incarcerated. He has drawn the blueprints for many ventures from corporate holding companies to clothing companies, to patents and apps all from the rich vault of creativity that rests within him.

"If time truly heals, to educate therewith shall truly bring about the dawning of a new day!"

Kirk A. Gaither II

Recommended Reading

Laws of Human Nature – Robert Greene
The Art of Seduction – Robert Greene
Mastery – Robert Greene
33 Strategies of War – Robert Greene
48 Laws of Power – Robert Greene
Mind is the Master: The Complete James Allen Treasury – James Allen
Art of War – Sun Tzu
On War – Carl von Clausewitz
Your Magic Power to be Rich – Napoleon Hill
The Everything Law of Attraction: Dream Dictionary – Cathleen O'Conner, PhD
The Secret History of Consciousness – Meg Blackburn Losey, Ph.D.
The Prosperity Bible: The Greatest Writings of All Time on the Secrets to Wealth and Prosperity – Napoleon Hill
Love is Letting Go of Fear – Gerald G. Jampolky, MD
How to Have Confidence and Power in Dealing with People – Les Giblin
The Secret of Body Language – Phillippe Turchet
The Everything Body Language Book – Shelly Hagan
Face Reading – Simon Brown
The Practice Art of Face Reading – Simon Brown

*Glorian (Gnostic) Collection/Gnostic Astrology – Samael Aun Weor
The Holy Bible (KJV,NKJV,NIV,GNT,GB,ASB,TGI)
Complete Book of Astrology – Kris Brandt Riske, MA
Moon Phase Astrology – Raven Kaldera
The Only Astrology Book You'll Ever Need – Joanna Martine Woolfolk
The Secret Teaching of All Ages – Manly P. Hall

Six Pillars of Self-Esteem – Nathaniel Branden
Bad Boys, Bad Men. Confronting Antisocial Personality Disorder (Sociopathy) – Donald W. Black, MD and C. Lindon Larson
Overcoming Anxiety for Dummies – Charles H. Elliott, PhD and Laura L. Smith, PhD
Depression for Dummies – Laura L. Smith, PhD and Charles H. Elliott, PhD
The Worry Cure: Seven Steps to Stop Worry from Stopping You – Robert L. Leahy, PhD
Coping with Family Stress – Kimberly Wood Gooden
The Complete Idiot's Guide to Managing Stress – Jeff Davidson
Boiling Point: Dealing with the Anger in Our Lives – Jane Middleton-Moz
Obsessive Compulsive Disorders: Treating and Understanding Crippling Habits – Steven Levenkron

How to Close a Deal Like Warren Buffett: Lessons from the World's Greatest Dealmaker – Tom Searcy and Henry DeVries

How to Get What you Want at Work: A Practical Guide to Improving Communication and Getting Results – John Gray, PhD

The 7 Principles of Public Speaking: Proven Methods from a PR Professional – Richard Zeoli

The Art of Selling Yourself: The Simple Step-by-Step Process for Success in Business and Life – Adam Riccobani and Daniel Callaghan

Instant Influence: How to Get Anyone to Do Anythin-- Fast – Michael V. Pantalon, PhD

The Yes Factor: Get What You Want. Say What You Mean. The Secrets of Persuasive Communication – Tonya Reiman

Verbal Judo: The Gentle Art of Persuasion – George J. Thompson, PhD and Jerry B. Jenkins

The Art of Closing Any Deal – James W. Pickens

Advertising, The Uneasy Persuasion – Michael Schudson

Zig Ziglar's Secrets of Closing the Sale – Zig Ziglar

How to Be a Gentleman: A Contemporary Guide to Common Courtesy – John Bridges

Rules for the Modern Man – Dylan Jones

How to Work a Room – Susan RoAne

The Operations Manual for Corporations – Michael Spadaccini

Start Your Own Business: The Only Startup Book You'll Ever Need – Entrepreneur Media Inc. (Staff)

Shark Tank: Jump Start Your Business: How to Launch and Grow a Business from Concept to Cash – Michael Parrish DuDell

Grow Your Handmade Business: How to Envision, Develop, and Sustain a Successful Creative Business – Kari Chapin

Starting from Scratch: Secrets from 21 Ordinary People Who Made the Entrepreneurial Leap – Wes Moss

Wholesale 101: A Guide to Product Sourcing for Entrepreneurs and Small Business Owners – Jason A. Prescott

---

The Truth About Money, 3rd Edition – Ric Edelman

The Smartest Money Book You'll Ever Read: Everything You Need to Know About Growing, Spending, and Enjoying Your Money – Daniel R. Solin

The New Rules of Money: 88 Simple Strategies for Financial Success Today – Ric Edeman

Warren Buffett Invests Like a Girl and Why You Should Too – LouAnn Lofton

The Smartest Portfolio You'll Ever Own: A Do-It-Yourself Breakthrough Strategy – Daniel R. Solin

Invest to Win: Earn and Keep Profits in Bull and Bear Markets – Toni Turner and Gordon Scott, CMT

The Money Game – Adam Smith

Economics Without Illusions: Debunking the Myths of Modern Capitalism- Joseph Heath

Where Does the Money Go?: Your Guided Tour to the Federal Budget Crisis – Scott Bittle and Jean Johnson

---

Accounting Demystified: Hard Stuff Made Easy, 2nd Edition – Leita Hart-Fanta, CPA

Financial Management, 3rd Edition – Jae K. Shim, PhD and Joel G. Siegel, PhD

The Art and Science of Dealing with Difficult People – David Brown

The Hands-Off Manager: How to Mentor People and Allow Them to Be Successful – Steve Chandler and Duane Black

The Personal MBA – Josh Kaufmann

The Way of the Shepherd: Seven Secrets to Managing Productive People – Dr. Kevin Leman and Bill Pentak

---

Thinking Like a Lawyer: An Introductory to Legal Reasoning - Kenneth J. Vandevelde

O'Connor's Texas Rules* Civil Trials 2009 (Texas Rules of Civil Procedure, Texas Rules of Evidence, Texas Rules of Appellate Procedure) – Michol O'Connor and Byron P. Davis

Blackstone Paralegal Studies Program v. 11-13 – Blackstone Legal Institute

Legal Guide for Small Businesses 2nd Edition – The American Bar Association

---

Wing Chun Martial Arts: Principles & Techniques – Yip Chun and Danny Conner

The Tao of Wing Chun: The History and Principles of China's Oldest Art - John Little

How to Develop Chi Power – William Cheung

Shaolin Kung Fu: The Original Training Techniques of the Shaolin Lohan Masters – donn F. Draeger and P'ng Chye Khim

---

The Millionaire Prisoner: How to Turn Your Prison Into a Stepping Stone to Success – Josh Kruger

The 50th Law – Curtis Jackson (50 Cent) and Robert Greene

Hustle Harder, Hustle Smarter – Curtis Jackson (50 Cent)

Rich Dad, Poor Dad – Robert Kiyosaki

Start Your Own Corporation (Rich Dad Advisors) – Garrett Sutton

Run Your Own Corporation (Rich Dad Advisors) – Garrett Sutton

How to Use Limited Liability Companies & Limited Partnerships 4th Edition – Garrett Sutton

The UCC Connection: How to Free Yourself from Legal Tyranny – David E. Robinson (NationalLibertyAlliance.org)

Self-Help/Inspirational/Body-Mind-Spirit

- Eagles don't flock and chickens don't fly!
- Inside oneself is the only ground where the seed of success can be planted...
- If a man has not built himself by the methods in which he requires of others, he cannot lead others by those methods.
- To have power is to empower!
- I'm so street smart, I'm book smart... I'm so book smart, I'm street smart. O' the wonders of simple understanding!
- When you don't know HOW to learn you always have to start over.
- Never send the wicked to gather the meal, and never send the righteous to take counsel with fools.
- Street smart means you can survive on the bottom. Book smart means you can survive on the top.
- If I know what you want, then I know how to give you what I want you to have.

In a world filled with the knowledge of good and evil, where common sense is the master of a lay people, knowing not "how" to think, but through dark arts directed in the way of "what" to think, so that they remain in the shackles of the common herd education..."self-education" stands as a pearl deep in the sea of simplicity. Self-education is the mountain that leads a man's mind to question, and the ability to question without opinion is the door to wisdom where with introspection into the deep recesses of one's own heart, character is born. With the birth of character the weeds of ego begin to be choked out and the personality stilled and washed clean so that it serves as a clear window pane to the soul of man. With the maturation of character, one begins to pierce the veil of the tree of death in the world and in oneself, leading man to the gift of good sense where the questions of who, what, where, and when are superseded by the questions of why, and ultimately of HOW. To ask how is to examine the places that make up the whole of a thing. It is to understand what is beneath the hands and face of the clock, to know what makes the clock tick.

"The fear of the Lord is the hatred of evil"… and to hate evil is to gain insight; to discern people, places, and things as they are in contrast and in distinction from what they appear to be. When a man has the courage of humility to ask "how" he not only begins to evolve in the capacity of his own mind but also comes to the seat of the judge where he is gifted with the challenge of creating his own thought unadulterated by the opinions and perspectives of others. It is here where he can pose questions from his own core in relation to things as they naturally are, and by this lead men from the lower rungs of commonality into greater realizations of themselves.

The author has herein posed questions for the reader to ponder in the recesses of his/her own heart with hope that each may be led into the halls of wisdom, and by thus to a higher realization of themselves, and to a union with the Creator… Amen!

"By my words have I established immortality"

The Philosopher's Stone

Special feature from the coming book

"Black Grapes: The Stretching of the Stem": If Black Lives Really Matter.

If Black Lives Really Matter

Of all the lives, and the lives from lives
For the separation of truth from lies, and one's
Blessed from the despised. Who is and who isn't and how do we tell where we fall on the pyramid or how we fit in the prism
When all we have is words unfilled by desperation and commitment?
Do black lives matter? I mean I hear the question being asked and
The statement being sworn but when I look abroad it all appears to be
Nothing more than an ugly thorn in the side of an already starved
Body of men and women unidentified to themselves and shunned except for
When it's time to die or bear the burden of another that said black skin
Could never be an "I". But again light from darkness and black ink from the
Writer's pen makes me question again…do black lives matter?
The authorities say of course when a bad guy is needed or when
good entertainment is sought but otherwise not at all unless you be salt.
Are we the salt? I think that we could be when all things are considered, but
What good does salt do when it thinks it's sugar?

If black lives really matter why we ain't helping our own? Why do we need

What's white to determine what's right? If black lives really matter, why do

we not know the histories and tales of our great Kings and Queens of Africa

and Egypt? Why is our whole existence wrapped up in the shortest month of the year

as a mockery to the shackles of our ancestors, and we sit quietly without

a word spoken? Does no one else feel the disrespect? If black lives really

matter why don't we get up off our lazy asses and go to work, put our

money together and let our neighborhoods look good. Why don't we stop killing

each other and take care of our babies?… Why don't we cut a G from our colorful

banner of shame and return to greeting each other as "my Niger" with full

knowledge of the honor and love of the Creator?

If black lives really matter let us quit raiding in a war not our own in the

Streets like fools and understand that we foreign, we not from here, our mother

Is across the waters. Let us soak up the gift of education and

Prosper because we're supposed to.

If black lives really matter quit being told what to do, throw down those

Compelled benefits and reserve your rights. If black lives really matter, why

We don't have unlimited credit? I guess you don't know that you have been held

Captive by our own high knowledge, and by the wisdom that you gave.

If black lives really matter quit playin' ghetto games and cloaking yourselves

in the uniform of a thief and unwanted stereotype. Oh you must not

Know that that bullshit was designed for you so you'd know just how much your

Lives matter… Just enough to tax, and shake down, just enough to lock up

and murder for the thrill, just enough to take yo bitch and yo babies and pimp them

under the arm of ol' Uncle Sam. Yeah nigger your lives matter just enough to

hate, and just enough to give all the poison you need to kill each other. Yeah

nigger your lives matter just enough to lie to about who you are. Did you

know that Jesus was black? And Adam was black? And Solomon is the son of

Osiris? Wait I know. Who are they, right?

I guess nobodies if you didn't know. I guess you also didn't know that the

Throne to the church and the state are yours and would be if your lives

Mattered. But don't blame me and don't blame them. That's why your lives don't

Matter now…you whine and complain too damn much and still don't know shit.

Your lives matter so much you are stupid to the phrase "man, know thyself"

But you got swagger though, you're cool as hell with your broke ass. They

Love you like that. You don't own nothing, and you are faithful to another's

Opinion of you, ain't you "good nigger." I'm telling you that your lives

Matter when you stand upright, get right-squared, walk it and

Start demanding so, with proper knowledge, of course. But then look what we

Have here…you little crooks gotta start reading books!

Can't be fooled when you know the authority, when you know the difference

Between laws and rules, and which applies to you and which don't and why.

Do black lives matter? I hope so! But this is a question and phrase that calls

for the protocols of responsibility. Damn god, don't you know that you the

temple of God? Don't you know that you are the epitome of what God literally

looks like walking on the earth? Don't you know that your father and mother to

all the people of the earth? Like hell you matter! That's why you get beat,

that's why you get raped, that's why you get murdered, that's why you're hated and cheated…because you matter! You forgot yourself and left the whole world

without its King and its Queen mother. You left creation astray and you

think somebody should pity that. I think not! Then you wouldn't be the blessing

that you are. Then you wouldn't be so needed. Then the whole world

wouldn't be waiting for its crown jewels to return to the top of the mountain

You fell the lowest because you stood the highest, now climb my brother and

Carry your sister atop your backs until you can hear the Father and don the

Cry of the amen. Ain't you God? Sure you are, so get up God, and act like it

The whole world is yours when you say so, but you can't be what you're not so

Get off that colorful shit and educate. It's not your skin, it's ignorance

That everyone hates, and being on the bottom when you come from the top says

That you acting dumber than everybody. You mean too much to give a helping

Hand. The whole house is yours, so rise Niger, and show us the King and the

Queen that history says you are, or you didn't know?

If black lives matter somebody would have told us so. Somebody would have kept

Record of all that you've done. Somebody would have built great things that surpass

The test of time. Somebody would have drawn his image in stone... If black

Lives matter someone would tell you so while you down and out. Some of y'all

Might of went against the grain. If black lives matter then trace your

Lineage to God and say so... My brothers and sisters, my sons and

Daughters, my mothers and father, if black lives matter the Creator would of

Chose dirt of your hue when He decided a home for Himself in the earth.

Wait a minute, I believe He did, because your lives matter!

The Philosopher's Stone

Special features from the coming book

"Amen: The Book of Eli."

The words of the Amen, the faithful and true witness, the beginning of God's creation.

The Lord says to my Lord: "Sit at my right hand until I make your enemies your footstool."

Far from the rising of the sun to its setting, my name will be great around the nations, and in every place incense will be offered to my name, and a pure offering, for my name will be great among the nations, says the Lord of Hosts.

…for I am a great King, says the Lord of Hosts, and my name will be feared among the nations.

The nations shall see our righteousness, and all the Kings your glory, and you shall be called by a new name that the mouth of the Lord will give.

The one who conquers, I will make him a pillar in the temple of my God. Never shall he go out of it, and I will write on him the name of my God, and the name of the city of my God, the new Jerusalem, which comes down from my God out of heaven, and my own new name.

Blessed be the Lord, the God of Israel, from everlasting to everlasting! Amen and Amen.

1) Dear Lord, I sought your face, I cried with a loud voice and you did not ignore me.

2) My heart lifted itself up unto you so that my being would become yours and you held me in your hands of strength.

3) My gift which you have given me, I hold up to you now.

4) I have prepared it and made it fit for the lost so that none whom you have called would be left astray.

5) With my own tears have you blessed and anointed this trumpet.

6) By your spirit did you move my mind to knowledge and my hands to instruct my heart to your wisdom.

7) Here is my gift Father. Look on and see that your word is good. Search it Lord and approve your own work which you have birthed through me.

8) Let your gift make room for me, ushering me before the lowly and the great so that every man eat from your hands the same.

9) Take your gift and plant your seeds of uprightness in the hearts and minds of all men.

10) Hallelujah! Amen.

And the peoples will bless the name of the Lord, for in one day He has cut off the head and the tail but reserved unto Himself a remnant whom He called by His name for they rejoice in His salvation.

And His house is founded securely upon the rock and its banner is the name of the Lord Christ Amen, forever and ever. Amen, Amen and Amen!

www.ingramcontent.com/pod-product-compliance
Lightning Source LLC
Chambersburg PA
CBHW060641150426
42811CB00078B/2245/J